I'll Try Tomorrow

ISBN 1-58898-529-6

I'll Try Tomorrow

Jeanie L.

greatunpublished.com
Title No. 529
2001

Dear Bobby, Danny,

I'll Try Tomorrow

*May the Grace of God
be with you always,*

*Your friend,
Jamie S.*

Reverend Martin D. McGrail, Jr., M.C.
Pastor
New Life Christian Church
Highlands, New Jersey

Some writers are more credible than others because of what they have lived through and triumphed over. Jeanie L. survived poverty, drugs, alcohol, bad decisions and a life of "invalidation." Today she is a living testimony of what God can do in the lives of those who seek him. Jeanie is a winner. She has made some important discoveries in her life... what Jeanie has learned from the adventure of living is powerful and leaves you with a postive new gusto for finding "validation" in your own life. After reading the story of Jean's life, you will want to reach out and celebrate sobriety and Jesus for eternity. I recommend this book to anyone who has ever wanted truth in the works of a new instrument of God.

To my parents, who are in a better place. To those who loved me when I couldn't love myself. Joe, who was there for me when I needed him the most. For my children, grandchildren and family, this is for you. For Nancy Heydt who helped me with her knowledge and understanding. Jeanie P. and Jeanine L. who told me to keep writing. And Lori C. who gave me support when I needed it.

MY PARENTS

On October 18,1942, I was born in an affluent neighborhood in Livingston, New Jersey. I was born in a little house that looked more like a shack. There wasn't any water, gas or electric in that house. We had a potbelly coal stove that was used by my mother to cook the meals and to heat the house. We had to pump the water from the outside well because we had no inside running water. For baths, we had only one large round tub that my mother also had to use to wash the clothes. We had an outhouse, a bathroom outside the house. Every few days, my father would throw in some lye in, to cover up the stench. I can still smell the stink of the place. Especially in the winter it was so cold out there, I hated to pull my pants down.

We didn't have any money for health insurance, so my mother had suffered giving birth to me in the house. She could have died because she had so many problems enduring the breach birth of my older sister. I was her third child and really should have been born in a hospital. She did have a mid-wife who helped deliver me. My father never believed in doctors. He was our only doctor when we got sick. I remember him making my mother always rub us down with Vicks and putting it in our mouths to make us swallow it. When I broke my leg, my father wrapped it in horse manure. It did heal, but I've never walked correctly since. Thank God, the three of us didn't die from some of these home remedies.

When I say affluent neighborhood, I didn't mean that we were affluent. We were the poor people, who lived in a small three-room shack down the hill from the rich people. There were three children in one room who slept in the one bed. My brother Sammy was the oldest and then my sister, Anna and I. Up on the hill, on the next block, there lived a man with his family, who I was told was in the Mafia, which meant that he was a racketeer, and our parents forbid us to go there. His house looked like a palace. He had a few small children around our age, who would come down the hill where we lived and play with us. Even though we weren't allowed to, we would sometimes go up to the big house to play. The man would allow us to ride his horses and play his pinball machines. His servant's quarters were larger than our whole house. I always felt so good when I was there. He would let the servants serve us cold drinks and sandwiches sometimes, which we really enjoyed. He was very nice to us kids, maybe he felt sorry for us. I used to dream of living there someday.

FATHER

There really wasn't any good reason for us to live the way we did, because my father, Frank, was a good mason and made decent money, when he worked. I believe he was self taught or learned from his father. He was a proud man and would drive me to many of the houses that he worked on and say "Look at that house, I did the brick steps or the brick front " In the summer he worked pretty steadily, but in the winter, jobs were often scarce. He never seemed to have money because he would spend it as fast as he made it, mostly on bills that were in arrear, from when he didn't work. His mother Sophie was born in a small town in Hungary and his father, George, was born in Czechoslovakia. They were both immigrants, who met and married in the United States. They both came to the States while they were teenagers. My father was born and raised in Sussex County, N.J. He lived on a farm with his family in Newton, N.J. As the oldest of twenty children, three of them had died at birth; he was the one who would have to leave school in the 5th grade to work and help to support his siblings. There were seventeen children, a lot of mouths to feed. My grandpa, George, was a hard worker too, but there were few jobs for immigrants, except for farming, and some masonry work. My grandmother, Sophie, later worked in a factory sewing parachutes, while the war was going on. She would let the older children take care of the younger ones.

FAMILY LIFE

Our family always seemed to be moving—like we were running away from something or somebody. I must have been very young, because I don't remember going to school. For many years, we lived in gypsy camps and other strange places. We lived in an old farmhouse, for a while, while my father worked as a farm hand. He took care of the sheep, milked the cows, picked up the chicken eggs, and fed the animals; my father said it was because of us kids always getting in trouble by playing with the animals that he lost that job. I remember teasing a goat with a pitchfork, or licking the cows salt bricks. I got a good beating for that. It was only a two-room shack that the owner let us live in, but it was warm enough, because we had a coal stove. After my father lost that job, we didn't have any place to stay, so we found other sleeping quarters. Some how we teamed up with the gypsy camps. I remember the dirty tents we slept in and the greasy food we ate when we lived with them. The gypsies were a funny bunch of people, they all stayed together like family. Some of them would dance into the night and wear a lot of beautiful jewelry. We would roast meat and potatoes over an open pit it, was always so good and tasty. They were good us, providing food when we were hungry, and shelter from the cold. I don't know how we survived living outside in the winter with only a bonfire to keep us warm. The gypsies were a bunch of tough people, how they were able to brave the elements year after year. We lived a kind of seesaw existence in those early days. It was never boring, but I developed feelings of deep insecurity. I remember that one of them tried to put his hands on me in a sexual way while we lived there, and how I screamed for someone to help me, but no one came. I did manage to get away from the man, but I never got over the feeling of being violated. Even as the years passed I still held on to that feeling. I felt dirty and unclean many times after that when I would be intimate with someone.

Us children must have gone to school by this time, but I can't remember any thing about it.

By the time I was around nine years old, my mother and father were drinking a lot, I guess they were depressed about us living the way we were. I'm sure they drank to alter their mental state or lessen feelings of unhappiness and were probably considered escape drinkers, or maybe they were really alcoholics. If they weren't, then each of them sure came close to living and acting like one. They always drank together and most of the time it appeared that they were happy and having fun. I couldn't wait to be able to drink and have fun to.

At times, when I noticed other families, I felt something was very wrong with ours. This was surely a dysfunctional family, but we didn't know it at that time. I never remember hearing the word," dysfunctional" back in the 50's or 60's. I had come to find out many years later that my father had been married to another woman, before he met my mother, and he was always afraid of being found. I don't think he ever divorced that other woman and he was afraid of what would happen if she found him. My father didn't have any children with this women, as far as I know.

MOTHER

My father and mother were both overweight and it seemed to me that it was hereditary—it certainly was when it came to Anna and me. Sammy was just the opposite, he was too skinny, seems he took after my fathers father. When my mother met my father, she was just barely five feet tall and weighed only 98 pounds. Mom was a beautiful woman who had wonderful full thick black hair that she wore in a bun or pushed up in a French twist, my sister and I also were blessed with that thick beautiful hair. She was raised in the old fashioned way by her Italian mothers mother. Grandmother, Rosa, was very strict and didn't allow her, to go out with boys on dates, or wear makeup. My mothers name was Grace, but friends and family called her Dolly because she was so pretty. She always wore big beautiful hats and kept herself nicely dressed. Her grandmother was a seamstress, who had been taught by her mother, so she made clothes for her. She never talked about her parents so I knew nothing about them. I often tried to ask her, but she avoided the issue .I don't know where her grandmother was born in the States or in Italy. Mother never talked about her grandfather or said where he was or where he was born. I understood from what my mother said, is that she felt abandoned and not really wanted by her grandmother and couldn't wait to get out of the house. She didn't have much education, maybe 8th grade and no job skills that I knew about, so she was stuck. I'm not even sure how she met my father; she just never talked about it. She would only say that he was so handsome and that she fell in love with him. I think he sweep her off her feet, because he was older, had a job and she wanted to get away from her grandmother. I believe that was the reason my mother left the home so young, to go with my father.

AUNT PATTI

I knew I had some Aunts and Uncles on her side of the family, but we didn't see them very often.

I did have the opportunity to meet my one Aunt Patti who was a professional singer, when I was around 12 years old. She was married to an older rich lawyer; Nick and had a beautiful home in Newark, New Jersey. She had paid me to go to Atlantic City with them to watch her child, at a fancy hotel, where she was singing in a big nightclub. After she had gotten dressed and stepped out of her room, I remember thinking that I had never seen anyone so sophisticated and beautiful in my life. Her dress must have cost more money than I could make in ten years. That week was wonderful, something I never forgot. The great restaurants that we ate in and the nice things she brought her child and I were unbelievable. Plus the maid service was nice and we could order anything we wanted from room service. Even when we went back to stay at her house for the rest of the week, she would get all dressed up, just to take me to the movies and to go food shopping. I had never seen anyone do that before. She even had someone come in to clean her house and tend her gardens. She had beautiful marble statues in the house and thick plush carpeting on the floor. The place smelled like money. I knew I would like to live like this when I grew up. Her and her husband were real classy people. For whatever reason, I was never invited to visit them again.

Maybe my mother was just ashamed of the way we lived, that's why we didn't see anyone in her family. I think she married the first man she met. My father was a big, tall good-looking man, clean-shaven, black hair and wore a mustache. He had a job, which meant independence for my mother. She was the woman who would give birth to me and be my mother.

MY SIBLINGS

My brother is three years older and my sister is two years older. We were all born in the same month, October, 18th, 20th, and 27th. My brother was the oldest, three years older, and my sister, was two years older than me. My brother started working at various jobs when he was around eleven years old. He would deliver papers, rake peoples leaves, or work with my father doing masonry work. He knew if he wanted something, he would have to go out and earn money to get it. He became a workaholic, working for many years for one company and at the same time running his own business That is why he grew up to be very successful in life. He was my father's mother's favorite grandchild, because she said he would learn to be a hard worker and do well in life and he did. My sister was pretty much the same way. She was the one who would get nervous when my mother would holler at her for sometimes doing things she hadn't done. My mother would apologize and say it was "that time of the month." When I look back on my childhood it's a wonder how any of us kids survived it at all. The poverty plus the father and a mother who always seemed to be defeated by society. My sister was very beautiful, but didn't go out on dates too often. She had met a good-looking guy, John, fell in love and got married at age 17. Then my brother did the same thing at age 18. My sister was to have five kids and my brother has three. I don't ever remember either one of them drinking excessively, or getting into any trouble. I would bribe my sister, with promising her some new clothes if she would drive my friends and I to different stores to shop lift. She never lifted anything herself, only I stole. I was certainly the black sheep of the family, and I knew it.

It amazes me that we always had a lot of food, regardless of how or where we lived. We ate a lot of meat and starch, like potatoes, bread and sugar. I knew my parents drank alcohol sometimes, but I didn't know to what extent. My mother would get drunk on two or three drinks and start singing and dancing. I've seen my father drink a fifth of whiskey and still walk straight. I never thought of drinking as a problem. I always thought that people drank to get happy. I do know that my family life was messed up. I remember my mother always being sick with her hernia; she always had bad pains in her stomach. My father would say he couldn't go to work, because she needed him to stay home and help her. I guess that's why my grandmother didn't like my mother. She would say she held my father back, plus the fact that she was Italian, and grandma always had a low opinion of Italians. She said my mother made spaghetti and meatballs a lot, and my father was so big, 300 pounds that it was hard for him to work. As the oldest of 17 kids, he learned to do some cooking, especially his family's ethnic dishes, stuffed cabbage, and kielbasa, he was a good cook.

GRANDMOTHERS BASEMENT

When I was a few years old we had to go live in my grand mothers cold basement, for a long time, because we had no place to go. She always treated us with disrespect, like we were dirt under her feet. My grandmother would always threaten to call the welfare to have us kids removed from the house. I believe my mother was afraid of her. She was so controlling and us kids didn't like her too much either. She said that we were always dirty and that our hair was knotted, because my mother wasn't well, enough to keep us clean. Sometimes we didn't go to school because we didn't have clean clothes. My mother had to wash our clothes by hand because my grandmother wouldn't let her use the washing machine. I can still see her with that scrub board. I remember grandma trying to turn us against our mother by saying things about her, but we instead turned against her for saying those nasty things. I remember always being so cold. We didn't have too many blankets and the cellar was damp and cold. My mother would cover us with every coat in the house at night to keep us warm. We also had our body heat, because all us kids were still sharing one bed. Mom would make us say some kind of prayer, to ask God to help us get a place of our own. I don't think I could ever forget the fear I felt of the welfare coming to take us away from our parents and putting us in foster care. It was hard to sleep at night worrying about it. My grandmother was over 100 years old when she died, in 1980. She had out lived most of her children. She lived in Perth Amboy when I attended beauty school there in 1979 and I would go to her home and do her hair once a month. We had become friends through this time, but she still blamed my mother for many things, like the poverty we had lived in.

OUR OWN HOME

I remember my father coming home one day and telling my mother that he got a good job offer from a guy who lived in Southern Jersey. He said the guy had a bungalow that we could live in, and there was plenty of work for him and there was even a swimming pool, close by, for us kids. It was like a dream come true. We packed up what little we had and moved that week to Port Monmouth, NJ. We arrived, full of anticipation, to find a house that was so small we didn't know how we could even fit in it. Four rooms. That meant once again that we would all have to sleep together. Now I knew what they meant by a bungalow. It was a beach house that wasn't suitable for anyone to live in the wintertime. We had lived in worse places. At least we were away from the grandmother we hated. We all got unpacked and were ready for our new life. My mother deserved a break. She was grateful and happy, regardless of the situation. Again, she would try to get this to workout somehow. Us kids got registered for school in September. We even got some nice new clothes and shoes. My father was making some money now and he felt much better about himself. Us kids were able to go swimming every day and had a lot of fun. I even learned how to smoke cigarettes that summer from some of the kids I was hanging out with. It seemed funny at first because I became dizzy, but after a few times, I liked it. That winter came and once again we had a coal stove. It was all right because the place was small so it kept us warm enough. We finally had a home of our own. My father was even adding on another room, so we would have more room to sleep. This one night we were up late because we had heard reports on the radio about a North Eastern storm coming our way. It had been raining all day and the wind was blowing very hard that night. I could see that my parents were very upset. We finally got to sleep, but some thing woke us up. There was a loud noise and we all got up to find that the water from the sea was in the whole house. No one had told us that we lived in a flood area. I had never seen a flood up till that time. We lost everything that night, clothes, furniture, food, any important papers, plus any childhood pictures we had. My poor mother, who was only five feet tall, had the water almost up to her neck. We were removed in rowboats and taken to the local school on higher ground. We were right back to where we started. We felt defeated again. That was only the first flood. We had many more through the years we lived there. Over and over we needed to get food and clothes from the Salvation Army and the township. If there was a God, why did He cause these things to happen to good people? Why didn't He have any mercy on us? We had no other place to go, so we stayed there. We had even started going to a Protestant church, by now, but I had never had any lasting contact with any kind of religion. I was convinced that there wasn't any God. Not in our lives anyway! Till this day, I'm still terrified of hurricanes. When I got flooded many years later, in my own home, I went into a terrible depression. I had relived my worst nightmare once again and had lost everything.

MY DRINKING BEGINS

I loved the feeling I got the first time I had a drink of whiskey at age 10. It made me feel pretty and sociable like everyone else. I had found what was missing, in my life. My friends and I had stolen the whiskey from the local liquor store, it was called Apple Jack, and we were just hung out on the corner drinking and singing. Later on that night I threw up my guts, and was so sick, but I remembered the warm feeling going into my entire being and knew that I would pay the price to do this again. I know that my mother always gave me whiskey, for my toothaches or earaches. She would rub it on my gums and the pain would go away. I guess that left a lasting impression, because I grew up, much of my drinking was to stop the pain and to make me think I was as good as anyone else. I never had the nice clothes that other kids had, everything was given to us from the Salvation Army, welfare, or hand me downs. I learned at an early age, that when I drank, I could steal my clothes and look as good as anyone else. I didn't feel poor anymore. Most of my life was lived trying to act better than what I was. I didn't want anyone to know that I was insecure and unhappy most of the time. All that bitterness in me, made me act out so badly towards others who had more than I did. When I was in grammar school, eighth grade, I played hooky almost every day, in order to hitch hike up to Red Bank, N.J with the same four friends to steal clothes. There were so many beautiful shops and nice things, there for the taking. Stealing clothes became an obsession with me, I couldn't get enough. I stole even when I didn't need anything. I partied up through the second year of high school, ruining my chances of getting decent grades. I rarely picked up a book. Most of my friends went on with their lives and I found other kids who wanted to drink like me. Consequently, my life went to hell in a hurry. I always liked to be the leader of the gang, which I certainly paid the price for, as I got older. My mother always seemed to deny the fact that I was a thief even when I stole a car, and my parents had to come to the local jailhouse, in Keansburg, to get me out or when I would come home with beautiful articles of clothing almost daily. I would tell her that I had saved up the money. I know that she was in her own denial, just like I was. I justified everything I did. I had learned to manipulate very early in my life. I think she really believed most of what I told her. Even though she rarely went out, my mother always had on a clean apron and dress every day. She knew we were poor and were tired of wearing hand me downs, but she always washed and ironed our clothes so we would look nice. She wanted to believe the best about me, and protect me. Even when I didn't go to school and the Truant Officer came to the house, she would say I wasn't there, while I hid in the bathroom. She liked when I stayed home and smoked cigarettes with her. I think she was a lonely women, because she rarely went out anywhere without my father. Even with him, it was very rare. She did have one friend, who looked like a man, who used to come and drink coffee with her sometimes. I had never before seen a woman look like that. When I asked my mother about her, she said the women was just a hillbilly and that's the way she liked to dress. She was probably lonely too. My most memorable times with my mother were when we would have a few beers and sing and dance for hours. She liked to sing Italian songs and loved "Some one of these days" she sounded like Sophie Tucker. I believe my love for singing came from my mother. I also loved to wash and set her hair, than comb it out, and it would look so beautiful. Maybe that's why I did so well in Cosmetology School, many years later. We also liked to play Bingo for pennies. I only remember her playing soft ball with me once. I don't remember my father playing any games with us kids, but I do remember going fishing with him.

REFORM SCHOOL

I was having a lot of problems in school. All I thought about all day was where, how and when I would be able to get a drink. When I got to the ninth grade I refused to go to school anymore. I was stealing my liquor on a daily basis now and drinking a lot. I would take a soda bottle back to the liquor store for the 5 cents deposit and walk out with two bottles of whatever I could steal. Whiskey, wine or blackberry brandy. My friends and I would stand on the corner get drunk, throw up and sing songs we thought we were so cool. Some of us would even pee our pants, but we thought that was cool too.

Because of her lack of insurance and the weight, Mom never was able to have her operation. Every time she tried to lose weight, my father would tell her to make spaghetti sauce and eat, because she wasn't fat. I had started to smoke and drink at such an early age. By the time I was 11 or 12 years old was now having, what I called memory loses at that time. I know today that they were blackouts from the booze. A black out is when you act like you know what your doing, but you don't remember what you said or did the next day. There's a big difference between passing out and a blackout. When I used to live in Livingston, I would tell everyone, that I lived up on the hill and that the Mafia guy was my father. I said that all I wanted to be in life was a gun moll, and I almost accomplished that in my many years of screwing up my life. Between the drinking, shoplifting, and not going to school, I got in big trouble. The principal said, it's either go to school or go to court and take my chances. The school had given me many chances to repent and change my ways, but I wasn't ready for their discipline. I remember that day in court, like it was yesterday. My family was there, and I remember everyone, my mother, father, sister and brother all crying. The pain that I was putting them through could be seen, not only by me, but the entire courtroom including the judge. He sentenced me to six months, on good behavior, to Trenton State Home for girls. Which meant if I didn't get into any trouble, I would only serve that much time. My sister and brother were embarrassed for me and for themselves. That was in 1957. I was 15 years old. Being sent to reform school was a way of my growing up fast. I was to learn some things that I certainly should not have known at that age. I was put on ten days quarantine, after I arrived. That was the routine for all new inmates. That meant keeping me isolated from the others until they checked me for any disease or head-lice. Well, I had to show everyone that I wasn't scared so, while sitting in my cell, I decided that I would plan my escape. I was only there five days, but was able to talk to the other girls while still on quarantine. The escape attempt was ridiculous and of course was a disaster. I called the matron and said I had to go to the bathroom. When she opened my cell, I attacked her with a piece of plastic that I broke off from my mirror. I took her keys and went to open the cells of the other nine girls, who said they were going with me. Much to my surprise, no one came out of their cells. Well, here I was ready to get out and party. I had my beautiful long brown hair combed and my makeup on and it looked like I wasn't going anywhere. I had a choice, either run for it, even though I had no idea where I was, or where I'd go or run back into my cell. The matron had knocked the phone off the wall and started to scream, by this time. I heard the guards running up the steps that scared the hell out of me. I ran into my cell and closed the door, real fast. Talk about denial, after I heard the guards taking out the other girls, of the cells I had opened, I figured they forgot about me, so I decided to try to go to sleep. I guess they decided to save the best for last. When they came for me, they were really mad, as if to say, why was I making them do extra work? Like, this shouldn't be happening in the middle of the night. There were two big men, one who later on I got to know him as Mighty Joe Young. They opened my cell; they grabbed me by my hair and dragged me down the cement steps, and across the field to the punishment cottage. I can still remember my head hitting every cement step; I thought it would break open. It was raining that night and even though they had a car, they didn't use it, they were out for blood and they got it. They dragged me across the field by my hair, and than they would stop long enough to beat me with their fists. I thought I was in a nightmare; I felt like an animal and fought like one. The more I fought, the more they beat me. By the time I arrived at the cottage, I was soaked in blood and mud. They opened up the door to this small room and I remember thinking, at least there was a bed. Well, not for long. One of the guards went into the room, closed up the tiny bed, and threw it out into the hallway, than threw me inside. I still remember how cold I was that night. It was the middle of January. I had to sleep on the cement floor. They wouldn't even give me a blanket, sheet or anything else, for that matter. I only had on a pair of slacks and a shirt. That was to be the beginning of the longest night of my life. There wasn't any lights on the hall, just a lot of dark shadows of people moving back and forth. Maybe, because, I was always cold as a kid, that night and the many to follow were almost unbearable. The next morning, the matron came to take me to the infirmary because my head and body were full of blood. I gave her no trouble at all. I knew I needed help. The doctor washed me up and gave me eight stitches on top of my head and put ointment on my other bruises. They let me take a shower to clean myself, which made me feel much better. When I got back to my cell the matron brought me a tray with food, I told her to shove it, and leave me alone. I was really hungry. After that; it was bread and water, twice a day, for what seemed forever. Twice a week I would receive some food. Slop I called it, but I ate it. I stayed in the punishment cottage for three months. The solitary confinement was a very lonely time for me. I passed the time by thinking of ways to get even with society. I couldn't see my parents for those three months. I could only talk to the matrons who were all women, and really didn't want to talk to me. They finally gave me some blankets and a pillow. After one month they gave me back my cot. There was a dresser that I used as a desk. The matrons had given me pencils and crayons, with some paper that I could draw on. The smell of the place was bad, like body stink. We were allowed to take a shower once a day, only if we wanted to, I think some of those girls were afraid of soap and water. I never knew what day or time it was, and I never asked. I knew I wasn't going any place. They allowed me outside for two hours a day for exercise. Some of the others that were on solitarily confinement would get out and we would play kickball or softball. Sometimes we just played cards. I'd have to say that we were a depressed bunch of girls. I slept a lot to pass the time. After three months I think I got used to this way of living because it didn't seem to bother me as much. If you had never experienced, the loneliness of imprisonment, the agony and the pangs of starvation, then you couldn't understand the way I felt. From that first night I was always full of anger, rage and revenge, I think those attributes is what got me through those first months. I know I wanted revenge against society, the people who put me here. There was talk, from the matrons about them sending me to Clinton State Prison, but because I was only 15 years old, they couldn't do it. They seemed to know that I was nothing but trouble. When I finally got released, from the punishment cottage I was with the 'in" crowd, because of the stuff I had already done, and I had a gotten a reputation for being tough. I was still just a new face on the campus. The Butches, as the so-called men were called and the Fems, the woman, were looking to see which way I would go, and whom I would go with. This was slang for the Lesbian population. They called it, "The Campus," like we were away at a fancy boarding school. Not that I was any prize-package to begin with, but I was naïve, about a lot of things that I was seeing and hearing at the Reform School. I was now living with about 200-250 girls, between the ages of thirteen and eighteen. Many of them had been living on the streets, selling their bodies, shooting dope, or other illegal stuff. They had been around the block, so to speak. They already knew how to rip people off and how to apply their tricks of the trade. Most of the girls were from Atlantic City or Newark. Some were run aways and would tell me what they had to do to survive. I was getting one hell of an education, about crime and what happens on the streets. Some of the girls talked about incest within their families, with their Father or Uncles. I thought that had to be the worse of any kind of violation to happen to a person. When I reached 16 years old, I could have 2 cigarettes a day. If we were lucky we could steal them out of the closets while working in that area when the matron left the door unlocked. We were not allowed matches, but when we had one match we learned how to split the match in half, so we could use it twice. The black girls were the majority. The way I liked to dance and the way I could sing, I started to feel like I was a black girl in a white body. I knew I was in the right place. I figured I should make myself comfortable because I would be there for a while. I never cried over anything, except sometimes at night when I was alone I would cry and ask God, why He did this to me.

NO EARLY RELEASE

When I came up for parole in six months, they would not release me. That was to happen only if I was on good behavior. There wasn't much of a chance of that happening in this hellhole! The board said I had to get rehabilitated first. I didn't have a lawyer, but it wouldn't have made any difference, because I was guilty of bad conduct. There weren't any activities there that would change that behavior either. Except for school, where I didn't learn much, or all the hard work I did, that didn't help me to get rehabilitated. It seemed that every bad thing that happened, I was involved in. There were a lot of fights and the "family business" ran rampant. Most inmates had others who acted as her father, mother, sister and brothers. Most also had husbands and wives. They would have sex in each other's rooms or sometimes displayed their love for each other in the recreation room in front of everyone. No one seemed to care, not even the matrons. And the showers were a bad place to be; all forms of sex went on in there. I felt that a lot of the women were just lonely for their families, because some of them never got visitors. Most of the girls acted like they were lesbians, maybe they were. I figured they missed their boyfriends and did what they had to do to have sexual relations. I didn't like any form of intimacy to begin with, especially that kind, so I acted real tough so no one would bother me. There was one girl, a Butch, who tried to attack me in the shower room while I was taking my shower in the evening. She had tried to touch me in a way that was sexual. I was soaked with soap and water. We wrestled on the wet floor. She bit her teeth into the fleshy part of my stomach and drew blood. I pulled her hair and beat her head on the cement floor until she was bleeding too. A few of the other girls tried to jump into the fight, but were separated by the matron. Then it seemed like all hell broke loose and everyone was fighting. I think everyone there was filled with the same rage that I felt inside me. It probably would have looked funny if someone had a camera and was taking pictures. Most the girls were slipping and sliding in the water from the showers and a lot of them were bleeding. Some of us were taken to the infirmary for medical care. My stomach really hurt. I had those teeth marks on me for a long time. The girl that attacked me had a slight concussion, but she would live. I was never bothered by anyone after that incident. Of course the matrons reported this to the head of the school, Mrs. Shelly, but the girls parents also reported me. I tried to explain what had happened, but I wasn't believed because of my prior acting out and trying to escape. They said I was incorrigible but they had to keep me there, because I was only 15, and there wasn't any other place to send me. You would think I was a murderer, the way I was treated. Even the matron looked like a lesbian. I hated to have to wash up in the mornings in front of her; she always seemed to be watching me when I was half-naked. I knew by that time, after getting my head busted and spending time in solitary confinement, that I would have to watch my step if I was going to survive this place.

WORSE OFF

When I first got there, I didn't know half of what I knew now, and it wasn't a good thing. I was only guilty of drinking, stealing and being poor! I hadn't done anything like most of these girls. I think I thought I was a bit unique, because of this. I mean I had never sold myself for money or cashed bad checks, or stolen a men's wallet, at lest not yet! I believed that I was worse off than I've ever been. And I become a lot harder and tougher, by playing their games and always trying to be a hot shot. I could talk my way out of mostly anything, and could manipulate these women because I had a strong, outgoing personality. At the same time I had learned to build walls between me the others so they never got to know the insecure person I really was and leave me to myself.

I had heard it said that crisis changes people and turns ordinary people into wiser and more responsible ones. In my case I believe I turned into a sneaky, manipulating, self-serving person, an attitude that would help shape the rest of my life. Only the strong survived in this world, so be it. I started to work in the kitchen and sometimes have to pluck the chickens for our dinner. it was a dirty kitchen job. I didn't eat chicken for four years after I got released, it would turn my stomach. I would take the wine vinegar we used for salads and hide it for one whole month, then drink the whole gallon, thinking it was fermented and would get me high. The only thing it did was make me sick I drank perfume, 6oz. bottles (that we could buy for 25 cents at the store once a month) because it had alcohol in it, and it would burn so bad going down my throat, but I would do it every chance I got. Any form of cooking extract was good for a buzz too. Years later, when I drank homemade uncut corn liquor, it burned going down, just like the perfume did. I knew there was something wrong with me but I didn't know what. I worked in the laundry and waited tables for the employees that ate there. I know that I had a problem because all I could ever think about was when I got out I could drink and get high. I believe I've been an alcoholic since I was very young. Maybe from the first drink. Was my progression that fast? Why? How? When? It really doesn't matter. The main thing is that I knew what I needed to do, to forget the pain, anguish and shame in my life, is to drink my self into oblivion. This story is about rebirth, renewal and recovery.

GOING HOME

I was paroled in 1959 at the age of 17, after serving 18 months. I cried at that time because I had gotten so use to living the way I was, that I didn't really want to leave. There was a certain security about doing the same things every day, plus I would now miss all my friends. I knew how to survive there now, and the thought of " freedom " as we called it was very scary to me. How would I survive on the outside? I had to report to my parole officer for three years, and keep clean from any trouble. The social worker for the state home had made plans for my release beforehand and I was to go live with my sister and her husband in South Plainfield, N.J, where I proceeded to make her life a living hell. She had been married at a young age to a man she adored. They just had their first child, when I came along. The problem was that no one could control me. My parents certainly couldn't handle me, even though every month for those eighteen months they had come up to see me with packages of goodies for me and the other girls. They had to travel a long distance to get there so it certainly wasn't any fun for them. My parents could not just focus on my behaviors they had to take care of themselves. Plus with my mother being sick, she couldn't do anymore for me. My sister's husband was a top hair stylist and did very well in his field. The only problem was that he drank the way I drank, which meant trouble. I believe that my sister felt sorry for me and thought I would be some help to her with the baby and the housework. I wasn't, any good with babies and I felt I did enough work in reform school, so I didn't do much of anything for her. I got a job in a restaurant because I had learned to wait on tables in the reform school. I was also a parolee, so I had to have a job. I met the undesirables, like myself who liked to go to New York to party, because you only had to be age eighteen to drink. I wasn't allowed out of New Jersey according to my parole officer, but that wasn't going to stop me from going. I was always belligerent and liked to do things my way, regardless of the consequences, which was evident. This kind of thinking always got me in trouble. I would pay the price for my, so called fun, many times over. I loved being free, after being told, when to get up, go to sleep, what to eat and when to go to the bathroom .I was a free agent and would show everyone just how cool I was. It seemed that I always had the personality to attach the wrong kind of people. I was a pretty woman, with real long, rich brown hair, and nice hazel green eye. My shape wasn't bad either. I wore a size 10. Five feet, four inches tall and one hundred and twenty pounds. I wouldn't eat all week, except for coffee and toast, than eat a hot fudge sundae, in order to stay that size. . When I went to New York with some new friends that I met at the bar, we would go to Greenwich Village and drink and dance with the homosexuals. I had a lot of fun and I didn't have to worry about getting molested. In Harlem you could dance on the tables and party with the best, meaning the blacks, the soul people. I danced like a black person, meaning when I danced, I danced with a lot of feelings. Even when I dance today, people ask me where I learned to dance like that? I loved to sing and thought I might be discovered, while singing in Harlem. I always wanted to sing with the Oldie groups. I loved the Chantels, Little Anthony and the Imperials, the Drifters, the Five Satins, all the great Doo Wops, I did get a chance to sing in New Jersey in a nightclub, but by then I was a full-blown alcoholic, so was the owner, who wanted more than a singer. He was very wealthy, married and would do anything for me. That was short lived. I decided that to pay that price to sing was too much for me.

BEST FRIENDS

When I started to drink, as a kid, I had four best friends. Joyce came from a dysfunctional home whose mother was an alcoholic and never got sober. After her mother was in and out of many mental institutions, she died from alcoholic convulsions at an early age. Diana and Jean were sisters, and I was the kid their parents didn't want them to hang out with. Jeanine came from a good family, but they let her do want she wanted, which was hanging out with me and getting in trouble, she was a rebel. They thought that hanging out with me was exciting, until I got sent away. We would all stand on the corner and drink our wine or whatever we had stolen and think we were really something. I always sang lead, and they did the background harmony. Especially with the song "In the still of the night," by the Five Satins. And "Maybe" by the Chantels, those were my songs. For all I knew, we could really sing, but the booze had us screwed up. Years later when I finally got sober, I went to New York to see all the Do Wops shows that I never had the chance to see when I was drinking. I was always going but couldn't get off the bar stool to go! I kept going to New York, almost nightly now, after work. My sister and brother-in-law were on my back about the hours I was keeping. I'd get home at 6am and go to work at 7am. I wasn't doing very well. That drink had its hold on me and I knew I couldn't stop, I certainly didn't drink for the taste, I drank for the oblivion, it was the effect that I loved. I had become a desperation drinker.

MODEL

I had started be a hair model for the company my brother-in-law, John worked for. He cut all my hair short and would make it different colors and do it all different styles for these hair shows he did. I remember him winning some trophies for the best color and styling. We drank the same way. His drinking drove him to seek other woman who had the money to help him live the grandiose life-style he liked. He left my sister with five children and never returned.

My sister started to baby-sit Tessa and Phil's children after he left. Tessa had grown into a full-blown alcoholic by this time and wasn't capable of taking care of the kids. She started to form a deep relationship with Phil by this time. Together they raised his and her children and have been together for over twenty-five years now. My niece and nephews found their father after twenty plus years and talked to him over the phone. He lived in California for many years. He explained that he became an alcoholic and had lived a tough life, but that he was now sober for a few years, but he was sick with complications due to the drinking. Shortly after his phone calls to his children and after my sister sent him pictures of them, he passed away. My sister's children were always successful in working in their chosen lines of work. She taught them to get up early, get a job and work hard.

INTERTAINER

I was also singing at a club at this time. I used to wear matching colored clothes to compliment my different shades of colored hair. I thought I was really hot. Pink dress with Pink Chiffon color hair. I suppose I could have been, good, if I hadn't gotten myself so drunk every night. It got so that the guitarist had to hold me up to keep me from falling off the stage.

Boy, I was something else! I made $20.00 an hour and thought I was the greatest. That time in my life, like every thing else was short lived. I could never stick with anything because I had to take that first drink, I needed it. I had said earlier that I was a black out drinker, which means that I could be talking to you and never remember the next day what I did or said. You would think that most people would try to stop drinking at that point, I did just the opposite, and I drank more to forget what I didn't remember. It doesn't make sense, but nothing that I did made sense in those days. There is a saying in Alcoholics Anonymous they call it "self will, run riot". I did anything I wanted to, when I wanted. I didn't seem to have any feelings or regard for anyone else. I was selfish and self-centered and only cared about my own pleasure.

MY FIRST BOYFRIEND

I had a boyfriend, when I was only 14 years old. His name was Nicky and he was 18. He would drive to Staten Island to buy me booze. We had met at a bowling alley in Keansburg where they had a jukebox and a dance floor. He was a great dancer and we would do the jitterbug together, and everyone would clear the floor to watch. We would go to this wooded area called Scenic Drive and drink almost every night. That's where I lost my virginity. I got so scared; I got out of the car and ran though the woods, to get away from him. I didn't like sex or being intimate, even at that age. I did like to hug and kiss, but that's about all. What did I really know, anyway? I did know that I liked to get high, drunk, what ever, as long as I could feel better about myself. I had such a terrible opinion of myself at such an early age. Everyone would tell me how bad I was, and I loved it. I was always on the defensive, with people, and didn't trust anyone. I may have been suffering from a neurosis, an emotional disorder that arises due to unresolved conflicts. There were a lot of conflicts in my life that were caused mainly by me. I was the girl that other parents didn't want their daughters to hang out with. Even after I was sent to Reform School, my boyfriend would drive all the way there to see me. It didn't mean too much to me, but I liked all the candy and cookies, he brought for me, the, so I told him to keep coming. After I got released, we saw each other a few times and broke up. He said that I had gotten very hard in my ways and he didn't like it. He was such a nice guy, but I didn't want a nice guy. I wanted someone who drank and partied like me. Many years later I would see him and tell him that I finally stopped drinking. He hadn't changed much; he had married many years before and had five boys. I was really happy for him. I myself had never married all those years when I was drinking. I certainly didn't want anyone to tell me what to do, or interfere with my drinking. Like my former husband said, when I first met him "No one would ever marry you, because you are such a drunk." He married me after two years' sobriety.

RIPPING MEN OFF

I'm getting ahead of my self now. Let me go back to the good old days, or so I thought of them at that time. Little did I know that I would begin a journey into the worst nightmare of my life! By the time I was 18 or 19, I was drinking, ripping off people, stealing money off the bar, taking money from guys and making false promises like, " I'll meet you at a certain place, at such a time" and never show up. I also got good with a razor blade. I'd party with a guy, feed him extra whiskey in his drinks, help get him drunk and cut out his pockets, take his wallet out, take all his money and throw the wallet out. Whatever I had to do to keep my drinking going, that's what I did. I could just about work anymore and when I did, I was a waitress. I'd have to bring my pint of whiskey with me, in order to get to the job. I would start work at 8am. By 10am, I would have drunk all my booze and start shaking all over. All my phobia's would kick in and I would be paranoid of ever thing and every body, feeling like I would go into convulsions or jump out of my skin if I didn't get a drink. I certainly took more breaks than anyone else. I thought no one knew I was drinking especially when I drank vodka, that I thought you couldn't smell. But I reeked of booze; it was coming out of my pores through my skin. I was in such denial, that I couldn't see it and wouldn't have believed it at that time.

There was one customer, in the restaurant that I knew from the bar. He had a good job working for the South Plainfield Welfare department. He would always tell me that I was a good person, if only I would stop drinking so much. I knew I had to do that and get my life together. I couldn't figure out how he knew I drank too much. I do remember that he was a good tipper. He also told me he had seen me drink at my favorite watering hole and that I drank to fast. He suggested that if I slowed down, I might be all right.

UNMANAGEABLE

My drinking was causing my life to be completely unmanageable and out of hand. I had moved to Newark, New Jersey in 1962, after going there to check out the bar scene with a few of my friends. The night we visited, I went crazy with excitement. I loved it! Everyone was wild and carefree and didn't seem to care about anything but drinking and dancing. There were a lot of men and women who just kept buying me drinks. The women looked like lesbians, but who cared, as long as they didn't bother me in any way. I made sure I didn't go to the bathroom, when I thought any of them were in there. And if I had to go, I made sure it was fast. These were my kind of people, and I wanted more of this bar scene. I knew I had to get permission from my probation officer, in order to move to Newark and I knew I would somehow convince him that it was the right thing for me to do. I had been on parole for almost three years and almost ready to get off it. I told him that I had a friend who was a steady worker, Carol, a woman of good character, who didn't have a record, so she could help me be more steady and reliable. He did check her record and found her to be clean, so he allowed me to move with her. I was barely twenty years old. What he didn't know was that this woman was an active alcoholic and I had met her at a bar. She had a lot of her own problems, but she was my ticket to get to Newark. Boy, what a team we were!

We moved right to the heart of the bar area where we had gone that first night. It was the Lincoln Park area of Newark. The

Tequila Club and Jack's Star Bar were are favorite watering holes. Even though I wasn't of age to drink, I rarely was proofed at any bar. I thought I was the queen of the bar, being so young and pretty, compared to some of the older ladies that hung out there. Us ladies called the men "live wires" that meant that the guy had some money and didn't mind spending it on us. Or if they did mind, we would still get it, stealing it if we had to. I had drunk at the Army base in Fort Monmouth when I was only 14 years old, along with my friend Joyce who was eighteen and had a car to drive us there. I wouldn't dance with a soldier unless he brought me a drink. They used to say I was stuck up and hard to get. Between the long hair, the false eyelashes, and the beautiful clothes that I stole from the Red Bank stores, of course I looked a lot older.

Carol and I both got jobs, I worked in a Jewish restaurant and she got work in a plastics factory. Every day at 3:30pm, after I got off work I would go to the bar, to drink. And drink I did. It would amaze me that there were always so many people in the bar at that hour. I was also amazed that they all seemed to carry a lot of money. The girls would ask me if I wanted a drink and pull out $50 or $100 bills. I asked them what kind of work did they do? They would always laugh and say they were born rich or not say anything at all. I was still very naïve to the ways of the streets. It would take very little time to come to understand what was really going on.

Personally I really didn't care what anyone did to get their money, as long as they spent it on me. I never had to buy a drink in the bar; it seemed they were waiting for me. People said I had a good personality and was easy to get along with. Plus, as I said before, I was young and pretty, which helped a lot. There was never a shortage of men in these bars, they came to use us and we were there to use them.

I don't think I ever realized how young I was. I had missed most of my childhood, because I never did childish things. I don't even remember playing with dolls or girl stuff like that. I was a tomboy and liked to climb house roofs on the beach, again with the same friends and break into people's summer homes to steal what they had. Televisions, radios, dishes, silverware anything we could sell to make a buck. I even broke my leg jumping off a roof, to get away, but I still found that a lot more exciting than anything else I might do at that age. I always liked action, negative as it was in most cases.

GAMBLING

Years later, I got caught up in gambling, with the guys at the Italian American Club, where I would roll the dice and play cards, with someone else's money, of course. If I had a good night, who ever I was rolling the dice for, would give me some money, sometimes quite a lot. One thing about a gangster, they knew how to treat a lady. We would eat and drink together and enjoy ourselves. That really fed my ego and my grandiose behaviors. I think I may have suffered from megalomania, an abnormal preoccupation with delusions of grandeur, wealth and power. I don't remember them trying any thing sexual with me. They were real gentlemen. I did date one of them around that time, he was a compulsive gambler, and he was good to me. I thought his life was so exciting and I wanted to be just like him. Then when his poor Italian mother would cry to me and tell me how he was in trouble with the loan sharks an how they were going to break his legs if he didn't pay them on time. She even paid the loan sharks herself when he didn't have the money. He had also had served three years at Rahway prison for embezzlement. He told me he was always "chasing his money" to try to get even. I still wanted to be like him, but not get caught. Remember, I always wanted to be a gun moll, since I'm a small child. I thought I had the world by its tail and I was enjoying the free ride.

LOSING CONTROL

Meanwhile, the bars and drinking were getting to me. I was losing control. I was having blackouts almost every time I drank and waking up in strange places with strange people and not remembering how I got there. My roommate Carol had cut her wrists and had tried to jump off the second story roof while she was drunk, because of a bad relationship. A few years later she had wound up in a mental intuition because of her inappropriate behaviors. Like I said before, we were some team. Two alcoholics that refused to admit that we had a problem with alcohol. If only we had more money, if only we lived in a different area, if only we met the right soul mate, and on and on. We had a million excuses for our drinking. We figured if we moved to a different part of the city, we would feel better and not drink as much. It's called a geographical change. It just doesn't work if you're not ready. Within a few days of moving to a nice classy apartment in East Orange, N.J, I had a job in a Greek restaurant and the owners really seemed to like me. I had to walk a few blocks up the main street to catch the bus but that didn't seem like a problem. I had gone out and brought all new uniforms just for this job, because I had to look good. I didn't want them to think I was a drunk. The first day of trying to get to that job, became my biggest nightmare. While walking to the bus stop, I spotted a bar on the right hand side of the street. I didn't notice that City Hall was on the left. I had such a hangover from the night before that I decided to stop in the bar and have just one shot of whiskey and a beer. I thought that this time it would be different. Why? Because I had the beautiful new apartment, in a new neighborhood, the right job, and my life was going to be so great, I had no reason to screw up. Any way, after I ordered my drinks, a guy, at the bar ordered another for me, which I accepted, of course. Then it was blackout time. I don't remember anything until I came to, in a padded cell. I believe I had become delusional because I was telling the cops that my father was the mayor of Newark and I was going to have them all locked up. I passed out again and woke up in a drunk tank, tossing cigarettes to the other inmates, who were all men. They were calling me "wild one", plus other names I will not mention. They were also urinating in front of me, which really turned me off. Till this day, I can never understand why a young women, such as I was, would be subjected to such vile manners. I still wanted to be considered a lady, even after all this insane behavior. I was just an alcoholic completely out of control.

They held me overnight and the next morning, on Sept 26,1962, they handcuffed me to the men and took me to court. The judge must have thought I was worth saving for, instead of sending me to jail, he ordered me to go to AA for a year, and also to stay on probation to the court for that time. Alcoholics Anonymous, why? I had never heard of that place! He asked me what I wanted to do? Even then, I couldn't keep my big mouth shut. I blurted out, "What the hell do you think I want to do!" I didn't even know what Alcoholics Anonymous was. I figured, maybe it was a place, where they would teach me how to drink without any problems. When I asked someone what it was for, they said, that's a place where drunks gather together and pray. Like I didn't have enough problems! I did know, that the insane asylum lay ahead for me if I didn't do something.

First A.A meeting

I was ordered to report to my probation officer the night of my first meeting. His name was Archie and he looked like a guy I could get over on and make him forget all this A.A stuff. Well, I tried, but after he saw I'd been drinking, he said, "Come back next week, and try to be sober." I said, "You must be kidding. Sober! What's that? Something you eat?"

I had to go to a meeting every Tuesday night at 8pm, so on Monday nights I tried not to drink too much. It never worked. Archie would take one look at me and say "maybe next week you'll try harder". Meanwhile, I was watching the other members claiming they didn't drink—for one week, one month, 90 days, and I thought, "They're full of it! How could that be?" I had drunk with some of these guys on Mulberry Street, where I drank just like them. Many of us had drunk out of the same wine bottle and shared the same sleeping quarters. Mulberry Street was Newark's skid row like the Bowery was to New York. You could get drunk there on ten-cent beers and sleep in the alleys or anywhere you could find space. The cops didn't like it but they usually left the derelicts and the undesirables alone. Many of these derelicts were highly educated, held good jobs and had beautiful homes and families at one time. The disease of alcoholism and drug abuse had destroyed their relationships, their ability to work, they had lost everything, including them selves, and wound up living on the streets. The hideous part of being an alcoholic is that the worse off you get, the easier it is to accept that this is your destiny. How could they be sober, when I craved that drink every day to the extent that if I didn't get it, I would surely die? By this time I was a wino, someone who just lived to drink his or her wine, in order to survive life on a daily basis. Surely, nothing but a hospital and a hypodermic needle could relieve me from this terrible obsession. But there wasn't any hospital for me, so I had to keep the alcohol in my system to live. I no longer fought drinking as an escape rather I embraced it. I had given up the struggle. Things weren't going as I thought they should, for my greater enjoyment, comfort or fame; therefore, if the universe wouldn't play my way, I wouldn't play at all. The loneliness and my deep sense of personal failure were overwhelming; I even considered suicide to take me out of this life I was living.

When someone was getting a 90-day piece, for 90 days sobriety, I was so envious, devious and resentful that I would try to entice him or her to join me for dinner at my house, which consisted of a can of soup. But I certainly had alcohol all over the place. A drink, to celebrate their triumph over alcohol! Plus, if they really hadn't had a drink for 90 days, they would have a lot of money saved up to treat me to a few bottles of whiskey. Some times they drank, sometimes, they didn't. I always felt bad afterwards, if they did drink, because when I'd see them, back on the streets looking again like a bum, pan handling and trying to rip people off, having to go back on Welfare and sleep on the streets, I felt terrible. I myself had pan handled because I thought it was exciting, like getting something for nothing. I certainly wasn't proud of these games I played with human lives. I was so miserable with my own life, I wanted everyone to be miserable.

UNEMPLOYABLE

The AA people kept telling me that I could stop drinking, one day at a time, once I made a decision to get sober and learn how to stay sober. Again, I wouldn't listen. I knew how sick I was from the alcohol, but I wasn't ready to lose my best friend. Alcohol gave me my outgoing personality, my self-esteem, my friends, so I thought, until I became a recluse. I was unemployable by this time, I had to drink every day, and jobs were getting harder to get and keep. I didn't care whether I had a job or not. I knew it didn't make any difference where I started the inevitable end would be skid row and death. The people in A.A were telling me to just take it one day at a time. That it would take a lot of work and there would be some pain involved but now people like me would have something they deserved. I would have people who cared and complete instructions from my Higher Power on how live in my recovery.

Pregnant

I found out I was pregnant in 1963, when I was 21 years old. I felt happy about it. Maybe I thought a baby would straighten me out. I know today that, it doesn't work like that. The father of my baby was an Italian guy that I had known from my favorite hangout. I told you I was a blackout drinker, so I didn't remember that anything happened between us until after I woke up in his apartment. I knew that he was from Italy and that he was a hard working construction worker. I also knew he cared about me, but didn't like the way I drank. He had told me this in one of my sober moments, at the bar. Well, two months later, after not getting my period, I knew I was pregnant with his baby. The reason I knew that, is because I was not an intimate person, and really didn't like or have sexual relations unless I was drunk, when I couldn't feel anything. I had so many walls, between men, and me that I only used them for what I wanted, and they used me. I had been raped and beaten enough when I was drunk, that all I wanted to do is get even with them. When I was half-way sober, no one could get near me. I didn't like to get involved with anyone, no relationships, just me and my bottle. Those walls stayed up for most of my life, even after I got sober, I didn't have the capacity to love or care about anyone, not even myself. It took a long time to trust anyone. Because I was a clean drunk and always dressed nice, I thought I was all right, almost until the end. I didn't want everyone to know the truth about me so I tried to keep up appearances. I never got morning sickness, because

I had my mornings and nights all rolled into one. I went to the clinic to get prenatal care, at which time they told me I was a high risk. My blood pressure was high and I had toxemia. This had everything to do with my heavy drinking.

Bill

Bill was good looking: medium built, hazel eyes, and brown hair. He was a truck driver and a tough guy who didn't take any thing from anybody. He was a ladies man. He loved life and loved to drink. We knew each other from the bar scene and one night and after he broke up with his long-time girlfriend, we started seeing each other. He really seemed to like me. He had a little boy, who was with his former girlfriend, but who he seemed to love a lot. After getting together a few times, we found that we liked to drink the same way, and had a lot in common, so we started living together. He also loved children and the fact that I was pregnant, two months, didn't matter to him. It was because of him that I didn't terminate my pregnancy or put my son up for adoption. I still don't know if I could have done that but, but I had thoughts, only because I was scared of being alone and raising this baby by myself. He was really a decent guy and a hard worker when he was sober but that wasn't too often. He would go crazy when he drank, and we would see who could drink the most and get the drunkest. The jealously and the possessiveness was terrible. He would say that if he couldn't have me, no one could. He was also suicidal. He would slash his wrists open, all the time and say he wanted to die, if I left him. I couldn't count the times he did this to himself. Every time I thought it was the last time, because he would bleed so much and have to be taken to the hospital, to get stitched up. After each incident he would promise never to do it again. The doctors said that he might be suffering from a split personality. A dissociate disorder involving a sudden, temporary change in normal integrated functions of consciousness, identity or motor behavior, so that some part of one of these functions is lost. They recommended medication, but he refused. The doctors would threaten to put him in the psychiatric unit for observation, but he would walk out and leave the hospital. One moment he was one way, the next he was altogether different.

We both decided I could get a job for a while if I tried to cut down on my drinking. I did try really hard to stop for a while, but as soon I took that first drink, I couldn't stop. It became more and more necessary to escape from myself. My remorse, shame and humiliation when I was sober were almost unbearable. The only way existence was possible, was through rationalizing every sober moment and drinking myself into complete oblivion as often as I could. Bill already had a good job, so, he could pay the rent and the bills every month. He was a good provider when he was sober and deserved more than I could give him. Love was very hard for me to feel or to treat another person in a loving manner. I had never had any emotional maturity in my life. Its development had been arrested by my obsession with self, and my egocentricity had reached such proportions that anything outside my personal control was impossible for me to think about. I had been immersed in self-pity and resentments for too long. Bill would come home every payday with a bottle for us, and new clothes for the baby. I didn't know the first thing about a baby, but he did. He bought the crib, dresser and whatever else I needed. I worked at a restaurant as much as I could, when I wasn't to hung over. Now, I had an excuse, when I didn't go to work. I was pregnant and everyone knows that pregnant women get sick in the morning. I played that to the hilt! I was still seeing my probation officer, Archie, even though I was off probation by now. He kept trying to talk some sense into me about getting sober, but I wasn't ready to listen. Also, when I was in reform school, every night we would all stand up on the top of our dressers and say the Lord's Prayer through the top of our doors that were partly screened on top. I'm not sure to this day why we did that. Maybe we were told to, which was probably the case. For some reason I enjoyed doing that and promised myself that I would learn the other prayers, like the Hail Mary and Act of Contrition, which I did accomplish. That reform school habit stayed with me the rest of my life, when I wasn't too drunk, to say my prayers. I felt I had a sense of decency, even with the things I was doing wrong in my life. I used to pray what I know today as foxhole prayers, like "Please Lord, get me out of this one, and I won't do it again," or ", I'll really try tomorrow, if you give me another chance." No matter what our spiritual inclination, we tend to pray more fervently when we feel most threatened and helpless. But after things quiet down, our reliance on God diminishes and we go back to "handling" everything ourselves. The definition of insanity, as I know it today, is doing the same thing over and over again, looking for a different result. Every time I picked up that first drink, I thought it would be different, that the results of this drink would be different than the last. I was always playing catch-up when I drank, like I couldn't get enough. This obsessive-compulsive disorder took up all of my time, energy, and money. If I wasn't actually loaded, I was thinking about it, trying to get money for it, or trying to get straightened out. I was filled with despair, a distorted reflection of reality. I felt that if I could unreservedly ask God to help me, that I could then surrender and allow myself to be rejuvenated by God's power and grace. It seemed, right from the beginning, that with liquor I could always retire to my little private world where nobody could get at me to hurt me. It seems only fitting that when I did finally care about someone, it would be another alcoholic. For the next nine years, from 1964 until 1973, I progressed as rapidly as is humanly possible into what I believed to be hopeless alcoholism. Fear of rejection from society and its ensuing pain were not to be risked. I found a false courage in drinking. I didn't have the ability to love, feel, or care. I'm not even sure I had the capacity at that time in my life. I started to drink to live and live to drink; it was like being in a bottomless pit. There was just no end and I could see no way out.

A Baby boy

In the midst of this, I had a baby boy. I had such a hangover when I went to deliver him; I think the pain was greater than it normally is. I watched him being born in the mirror above the table where I just gave birth and I was amazed that such a wonderful miracle could happen to me. I felt true love for the first time in my life. I truly knew there was a God, to allow such a thing to happen. Now, I had responsibility and wasn't sure how to handle it. Bill was there with me at the hospital and was overjoyed that we had a baby boy. He loved the baby from day one. He brought the baby, little boy clothes and a teddy bear. I named him after another baby that was born on the same day to Afro-American women in the next bed because I didn't have a boys name picked out. She had named her son Anthony Marcus and I named my son Marcus Anthony. I thought it was such a beautiful name. He was born on July 16th, 1964, weighed 5 lbs. 14 oz. And was 22inches long. He was pre-mature and had to stay in the hospital a few extra days. That was caused mainly because of my drinking the doctor said. He had a head full of black curly hair, and was the most beautiful baby I had ever seen. . I vowed that I was going to be the best mother to this child. He was so tiny and needed me to give him the love and care that he deserved. I used to take the time to sing to him. My song for him was "You'll never walk alone." My life had been so full of deception and dishonesty, and I had broken most of God's laws, so why was He so good to me now? This baby gave me hope, but it didn't last long, for I had never had any emotional maturity and had just never grown up. I tried harder than ever to stop my drinking but it didn't work for me. So, being a mother had its drawbacks as far I was concerned, and the only people who would support this attitude or who I felt I understood me at all were the people I met in bars and the ones who drank as I did. It became more and more necessary to escape from myself, for again my remorse and shame and humiliation when I was sober was almost unbearable. My baby's father came to the house to see his son and I told him to get out! He never came back, but every month he sent $50 through the probation office to help support him. I was grateful that he did that for eighteen years. The probation office told me they never seen a father pay on time like he did. For many years I had lied to my son by telling him I was married to his father. It wasn't until he was a married man, at age 30, that I told him the truth. He said he knew all along but never spoke about it. He said he understood and it was all right, but there had to be closure. By this time my mother and father became the superintendents of the apartment building where I lived with Bill and my son. My mother watched him while I tried to work. Everything seemed to be going all right for a while. Even in the face of such glaringly obvious consequences as arrests, hospitalizations and destroyed relationships, practicing alcoholics and addicts refuse to acknowledge that there's a problem. I was trying to control my drinking, but anyone who knows anything about alcoholism, knows it's impossible, it doesn't last. This is called denial! It's not will power, it's want power and I didn't stay in control for long. Addiction is not freedom. The very nature of this disease and it's observed symptoms point to this fact. We addicts value personal freedom highly, perhaps because we want it so much and experience it so seldom in the progression of our illness. I knew that Skid row is not only a place; it's a state of mind. I know today that I needed a divine intervention. At certain times the alcoholic has no effective mental defense against the first drink. Except in rare cases, neither he nor any other human being can provide such a defense. His defense must come from a Higher Power. I know that I needed some spiritual solutions to my life, but I wasn't ready to trust Him. Most emphatically, I wish to say that any alcoholic capable of honestly facing his problems in the light of my experience can recover provided he does not close his mind to all spiritual concepts. He can only be defeated by an attitude of intolerance or belligerent denial. Willingness, honesty, and open mindedness are the essentials of my recovery, but these are indispensable.

Gambling More

Getting back to my family, out of the seventeen kids that my grandmother had, three of my Uncles that I know of, had some serious drinking and gambling problems. My Uncles, Bobby and Herbie were serious gamblers and Uncle George had psychiatric problems due to alcohol. In fact, the first time I gambled was at the racetrack; I had gone with my Uncle Bobby. Boy! How I loved the excitement and the thrills of it. Both my Uncles were high rollers and always seemed to have a lot of money in their pockets. It was both of them that showed me how to order lobster and fine wines. I always loved their grandiose behaviors. After a day at the track, they always took me to the finest restaurants and gave me pocket money. I loved this kind of recreation and the people who did it—the action people. This life-style is very addictive for many people. Many years later I discovered Atlantic City and loved to play the slot machines. I was now sober a few years, but I would get the same adrenaline rush I got when drugging. In fact I liked it so much that if I weren't careful, I could become a compulsive gambler. I believe that I could get addicted to the action, just like booze.

PARANOIA

I finally reached my breaking point when I got so sick from the booze. I had the shakes every morning, I sweat profusely, my blood pressure was very high, the paranoia was over-whelming, I was afraid of going out or staying in the house. I couldn't go out to the liquor stores anymore, unless I had a few drinks. I had a bout of paranoia while working in the restaurant and knew that I could never work at that job again. I did need to do something to earn some money. Bill paid all the bills, but I needed drinking money.

I got a job go-go dancing. I told you before that I always loved to dance and I was a good dancer, so it wasn't any problem getting jobs. I had to try out and show them how well I could dance and be pretty. Those were the only requirements needed. Back in the 60's when go-go dancing started, we looked at it as a true art form. I had all my costumes made. They were beautiful; mostly one-piece with lots of fringe .I loved the ambience of most of the bars that I worked. The attention from the customers, who admired my dancing skills, was unbelievable. The fast music that I danced to like, Wholly Bully gave me such an adrenaline rush. I usually worked three nights a week and made between $60 and $75 a night, plus tips—good pay back in 1965. The money was good, but I had to dance five hours straight, with three fifteen-minute breaks.

The bars I worked in had mostly married men and some women; out to have a few drinks for the evening, so I was rarely was bothered. There were bouncers who would help out, if someone did try to bother me. When I danced I hardly drank, it just wasn't allowed Dancing all those hours was hard work. and I had to stay in control so I wouldn't fall off the stage. I made up for it after the bar closed, by going to the after-hour bars to get my fill. I danced mostly in Newark and Elizabeth, where the ships docked and the hard-drinking seamen were good business in the local bars. I worked in Newark's Italian section, Down Neck, where a lot of racketeers lived, drank and gambled. Tips were always excellent in these bars. You could make between $100-200 on a good night. Something about dancing always made me feel better. I think it was the exercise, getting out of myself. Before I lost control of my drinking, I used to exercise daily.

Card games

During this time, I had a little sideline. I was also running card games in my house, where I could rip off the men when they got loaded, which became a regular thing. There was always a lot of alcohol available at my house that I charged for. The card games were fixed so that these men lost a lot of money. Bill and I would set them up to make them think they were winning at first, than we would raise the pot up to $100 ante, than raise $100-200 each hand. These guys would be so drunk; they didn't see the extra cards we held under the talble. These guys weren't the gangsters that I previously gambled with. I would never be able to get away with it. Those guys were too smart and street wise. These were your average hard workingmen who had just cashed their paychecks or had extra money in their wallets and wanted some excitement. They would chase their money, always thinking and hoping that the next hand was theirs, until there wasn't any left.

My boy friend Bill, who still lived with us, was now losing control of his drinking, which made it hard for him to work steady. We went to AA together but neither one of us could stop drinking. We had always known the dope addicts, who lived on the other side of town—dope addicts on one side of town, alcoholics on the other. One day we were so hung over and sick, we decided to go to the other side of town to see if this dope thing was any better. I had smoked marijuana a few times in my life and didn't like the affect on me, so I never did it again. I had taken some street pills, bennies, black beauties and a few pills that had no names. I did like speed or diet pills, so I could stay awake all night or clean my house. I would be scrubbing the walls at 3 o'clock in the morning or wouldn't go to sleep for three days at a time, but I had to drink with them for the desired effect. Talk about self–destruction, it was like I had the Devil in me.

Well, Bill and I did go to the other side of the city and sat with these addicts, who were mostly main lining heroin users. I thought, how horrible it looked, to have to stick a needle in your arm to get a buzz. Later, as the night went on, one of the addicts said, "Let me skin pop you." I didn't know what that meant, so I said I would try it, anything to help me stop the drinking. I did try it, and so did Bill, just for the hell of it. The rush to my brain was something I never experienced before. We both liked it, so it became part of our daily routine. We just didn't go home too much after that first time. I was too afraid of getting hooked on this stuff, so I only skin-popped twice a day. The dope cost $10.00 a bag and we did at least two bags a day. We "nodded out" most of the day. Meaning we were in a stupor like state. The sick, self-centered, and self-enclosed world of the addict hardly qualifies as a way of life; at best, perhaps it is a way to survive for a while. Even in this limited existence it is a way of despair, destruction and death. I knew I preferred my drinking to this dope. I was hooked on booze, which meant that even though I was skin-popping I needed to drink. Thank god,, I didn't get hooked on that stuff. Maybe because I didn't take it for that long a time. While I watched other people over dosing and dying right in front of me. I watched mothers there who would shoot up, with their babies, who didn't have any milk or food to eat. My son was lucky to be watched and fed by my parents. I was giving them my food stamps every month to feed him plus extra money for clothes and other necessities .The last day I ever took a drug, Bill had asked me to go home to take care of my baby, and get back to the AA program, so we could have a decent life. I told him to go to hell and leave me alone. He called the Narcotics cops to the house where we had been staying to get us busted or to get me to leave and go home. The Narcotics cops just checked my arms for tracks, that's needle marks, and didn't find any. When you skin pop drugs, you shot the drug into other parts of your body, leg, rear end, hand, or feet, not your main vein, so it doesn't leave any tracks or needle marks. After the cops left, all the guys in the house ganged up on Bill, because they knew that he called them and beat the hell out of him. I was too drugged up to help him. I must have blacked out or passed out, because the next morning, I received a call that Bill was dead. He either shot himself or was coming back to the house to threaten me to leave, or to kill me but the gun went off and killed him. The bullet went right through his heart. He was dead at the age of 31. No one but God knows exactly what happened, that morning. He had left his 8year old child, as well as my son and I. I found myself in the center of full-blown emotional upheaval. I went to the funeral, where I wasn't wanted, because his family said that I had killed him, which in many ways was true. I had never seen so much hate and grief at the same time. They threw me out of the funeral parlor, after I had viewed the body, but not before I put a letter up his suit jacket sleeve, saying how sorry I was for the things I did, and if he gets to heaven, to help me get there so I could be with him. I never needed an excuse to drink, but now I certainly had one. I never did another drug after his death, but I never stopped drinking.

Alcoholism is a hideous disease; it gets you spiritually, physically and mentally. It has no respect for race, religion, age, sex, education or socio-economic condition. It will hit those who least expect it, like priests, ministers, lawyers, and doctors. No one is exempt.

I knew there were only three alternatives, either get sober, die, or be in a mental institution for the rest of my life. I had heard this all at AA meetings, but I felt I couldn't stop. And what if, by the Grace of God, I could, and then surely my past would catch up to me. I was always projecting the worst. What if? How? Why? I always had an answer to why I couldn't or wouldn't stop. I do believe Bill had to die in order for me to live. Maybe this was his gift to me. Even though he drank, he had loved life and people to a great extent. But, he was sick like I was sick, with the same disease. He needed to be there to help me with my son, when I needed him so badly. For that I'll be eternally grateful. What a shame, that we sometimes need such bad things to happen before we can see the light.

Mother's death

Shortly after Bill's death, my mother got sick again with this hernia she had had for over 20 years. She was taken to the Newark City Hospital, because we still didn't have insurance. The hospital sent her home to soon after her hernia burst open, gangrene sent in and it was too late when she went back two weeks later. She lay in that hospital bed for three weeks asking for me, her youngest. Every night after dancing in the bar, I would call and ask my father how she was. He would tell me she was all right, even when she went into a coma. He was in his own denial. Because I was dancing and had begun to drink heavily after work every night, I was too sick and hung over and too ashamed to visit her. I never once went to the hospital to see her. My addiction insulated me away from people, places and things outside my own world of getting, using and finding ways to continue the process. The monotonous, imitative, ritualistic, compulsive, and obsessive routines of active addiction rendered me incapable of any responsive or meaningful thought or action. My father was watching my son every night and sometimes all day, because of the bad condition I was in from drinking. My parents still lived only downstairs from me, but there were days I never saw them or my son. I would pass out and sleep most of the day so I could go dance at night and start drinking all over again. Thank God, I knew my son was safe. He loved being with his grandpa, and was content and happy. I had always got along better with my mother, more so than my father. She always covered up for me from when I was a kid and started drinking. She was my biggest enabler, which she didn't realize, because she did it out of love for me. My sister-in-law and my sister came to my house one morning, while I was sick and hung over as usual, to tell me my mother had died that night, on December 22, 1967, without ever seeing me. They told me that her last dying thoughts and words were for me. She was forty-five years old and had had a tough life. Now there was another excuse to drink more. I always seemed to be strong in a crisis, so I helped arrange her funeral without much of a problem. I don't remember even taking a drink that day. But once it was over I couldn't stop drinking. Once again, how could I ever think of getting sober, now that I never said good-bye to the one of the two people I truly loved .Well, time goes by and we forget to remember what hurts us the most. We drink it away, or drug it away. I did continue to drink, because that's what I did best. That would keep away the pain of reality and the insanity that threatened my very soul, every waking hour of every day.

The Projects

Before long, my son was getting older and my father wanted to move away, more towards South Jersey by the seashore, He had been the care taker of the apartments where we lived for a few years. I had lived upstairs with Bill and Marcus. Now, without Bills income to help out with the rent I could no longer afford to live there. Welfare had told me, I was edible for an apartment at the Seth Boynton projects in Newark. I would be charged $40.00 a month, from my welfare check. Now, I was to live with other low-income people. As I came to realize later, that there were a lot of good people who lived there, who were just down on their luck, it was really a very nice apartment. I soon found out that not everyone drank like me, just because they were poor. My son, started school there, which was within walking distance from the house. He would walk every day with the other kids to school, so I didn't have to get up with him, which half the time I couldn't. God only knows what he wore or ate half the time. He was such a good boy, who would try to help me, when I was too drunk to walk or get up to get food if it was a day I was able to eat. He took a lot of abuse from me, both physical and emotionally, because I had so much anger, I took it out on him. Some times I would hit him for something that he didn't even do. His father had tried to see him again, but each time I threw him out of the house. Back in that day, to get child support, they went by the looks of the father and child. He looked just like his dad. I'm sorry today that I didn't let his father see him, because as the years went on, I had lost all track of him. I never had gotten his social security number, so that when I did try to find him, many years later, the probation department said they get rid of the cases after so many years, so there wasn't any way I could find him.

By this point in my life, I know that I needed a therapeutic community setting, such as a residential treatment center to dry me out and help me, but at that time I wasn't ready nor did I have the money or the insurance to go to one. I really needed to regard my drinking from a different perspective. It was no longer fun. I was now becoming a recluse. I believe that I suffered from some schizophrenic disorders, like paranoia, dependency, disorganization, and delusions at times. My fear was so great that I couldn't go out of the house without panicking. I even brought a $500.00 security dog, Caesar, which I ruined when I would let all the kids in the neighborhood; walk him, because I couldn't. This dog was supposed to protect me, but he never did. Finally he became so tame, that someone stole him and I never saw him again.

Soon after we moved in, I met a woman in the projects through my son who played with her children. Her name was Tessa and she was from Germany. She was married to a guy who liked to smoke marijuana and she loved to drink. Now I had someone close by to drink with every day. She also enabled me by going to the liquor store for me every day to get my booze. I had started to drink wine more now, because it was cheap. My son was becoming ashamed of me, and I was ashamed of myself. The people in the projects were talking about my drinking and me in general. My neighbor would call me all kinds of names from the window next door, which was only a few feet away from my kitchen. Her son used to come over and drink with me and would spend all his money on booze and she blamed me. I was full of fear, and wouldn't leave my house unless I really had to. I was a time bomb, waiting to go off. . When I say that I drank wine, I drank as much and as often as I could. Sometimes, I would drink 24 hours a day, black out, and keep drinking more. I had stopped everything social in my life. Now that I only paid $40 a month for rent, and got food stamps I could drink that cheap Boones Farm

Apple wine, as often as I needed it. I also had some friends, like Tessa, who would give me money or buy me the booze. I was disgusted by some and pitied by others. Marcus found out early in life that he had to survive, whichever way, he could. The neighbors fed him most of the time and he learned to stay out of my way. Any sober moments were used trying to make it up to him. I would buy him things, give him money for pizza, and let him go to the movies.

Blackouts

When I had dated, quite a while back, I made sure that the guy would have enough money to take me to a nice place for dinner and drinks. The problem was that by the time we usually had to wait for our table, I would be so drunk, from drinking all the drinks I had heard of on television like, slow gin fizz, manhattans, champagne cocktails, and anything else I had heard of, that I never did get to eat. And I'd forget who my date was and sometimes leave with someone else. Being a blackout drinker meant that I would come out of that blackout and be anywhere or with anyone, and not remember how I got there. The only reason I could still get a date was because I still was young and still pretty, and I tried to dress nice all the time and wear makeup well. I figured that's what made me a lady! After the first date, there was seldom a second. The guys used to say; "You would be so nice, if only you didn't drink like you do".

After awhile, I didn't care about dates and all that went with them, like paying attention to someone else for a while. I knew that my destiny was to drink myself to death and than, maybe I would be at peace or burned in hell, either one, it didn't matter anymore. The physical and mental agony was getting worse. Remorse and fear played a key role in how I felt about myself. I was always playing a role of being someone else, never myself. I would come out of a blackout and think that maybe the apartment caught on fire and my son was dead and be paranoid until I could get home from where ever I was. There were times that I said I would only have one drink and wound up, coming out of a blackout, beat up, raped or in jail. I still prayed, sometimes and asked God to help me, guide me, change me, let me be a decent person, "the way you would want me to be." It never worked for me because I was so busy doing my will, not His. I knew that if I could surrender spiritually, God would do for me what I couldn't do for myself. I believed that willingness and honesty were the key ingredients that I didn't have.

Joseph

Because I rarely left my apartment anymore, my friend Tessa suggested we take a ride down the shore, with her three kids and my son to go swimming. It was a beautiful hot summer day. We made sure we picked up a case of beer and a bottle of wine to keep us company, on the beach. We, of course, had to find a small beach, where we could drink without getting arrested, by the cops. We did find a small beach, in a small town, Union Beach, N.J where we had never been before. Anytime that I did go to the beach, I never went in the water, God forbid, I mess up my hair and makeup. The beach meant that the children could swim and have a good time, while we drank our booze. While Tessa and I were having a good time, doing what we did best, my son came running over to us, shouting to us to look at the beautiful Harley Davidson motorcycle that had just pulled up by the beach. We looked over and said that it was really nice, mainly to please him. I had always enjoyed riding on motorcycles when I did ride, which hadn't been for some time. A nice looking guy got off the bike and was now talking to my son, showing him some of the details of the bike. Then a light bulb went off in my head, because I was getting low on my wine, I could use a good stiff drink. I went over to the motorcyclist, and found out his name was Joe. He seemed like a nice guy and had spent some time talking to my son, who was really impressed with the motorcycle. I asked him if he'd like to take me to the bar, right on the beach, and buy me a drink. He just looked at me and said, 'don't you think you

had enough?" I told him we would have one drink and get to know
each other, and he went for it. Once inside the bar, I ordered a shot
of whiskey and a beer. He ordered a small beer and we talked for a
while. He said that he would drive me back to Newark on his bike, if
I wanted him to, and Tessa could drive back with the children. I told
him I would need for him to buy me a six-pack of beer to keep me
company and then I would go with him, which he did. By the time
we got to Newark, I was in and out of blackouts. When I came out
of it the next morning, this guy, Joe was sleeping on my couch, with
his boots on the floor, but was fully dressed and so was I. Something
happened to me that morning, I developed some respect for this guy,
because he didn't abuse me while I was drunk, and that was a first.
He asked me if I could make him a cup of coffee, I never drank coffee
anymore in the morning, I drank wine for breakfast. I proceeded
to find some coffee for him and some wine for me. I always hid
something to drink in my apartment, even though I lived alone with
my son, I guess I just hid it from myself., I knew I needed to always
have it on hand, so I wouldn't get too sick. While we were having our
'breakfast', I had lied to him, telling him that when I was married, I
didn't live like this, that we had a lot of money and a beautiful home.
He just looked at me and simply said, "No one would marry a drunk
like you and you're full of shit." I was actually insulted by the first
guy that I thought about respecting, and told him to get the hell out
of my house, giving him my phone number, on the way out. After he
left, I really had to think about the fact that he was the first guy to
see right through me and tell me the truth. Maybe, because he was
the first guy that didn't want anything from me. By the end of the
week, Joe called me and asked me if I would like to go motorcycle
riding that Sunday. I said, yes, even though afterwards I was paranoid
all week, just thinking about it. I even had got the courage to go out
and buy some new clothes. After all, I had to keep up appearances.
This guy had called me a drunk, right to my face, I had to show
him he was wrong. I found out later that Joe was 16 years older than
me. Maybe that's why he had so much insight into my life, I don't
really know. He certainly didn't look his age. He was a handsome

guy who had a kind heart and believed in strong family ties, values and common sense. I was looking forward to our date with both dread and anticipation. That whole week, I tried to cut down on my drinking, to sort of control it. It didn't work. By Sunday I was a nervous wreck, but the new clothes and the new make-up helped me to cover that up. Well, he came at 1pm, right on time as was planned and I was as ready as I would ever be. He wore his black leather jacket and looked real nice. I wore a blue tailored suit and black boots and also looked good. We were off to the seashore again. Boy! He certainly could drive that bike, so that I never got scared, even with those low curves, he knew what he was doing. We were quiet all the way, just enjoying the scenery. I was actually starting to feel better, or so I thought. By 3pm, I was starting to lose it, meaning I could feel my inner nerves crying out for a drink. I needed something to take the edge off. Joe asked me if I was hungry, at the same time I spotted the cocktail glass over top of the diner, which meant they served drinks. I said I was starving, but I really needed a drink. We got inside the diner and I was playing dumb, like asking the waitress, what's the name of that drink that has vodka and orange juice? The waitress told me it was called a screwdriver, and I ordered one. Joe ordered coffee. I told him I wasn't ready to order, that I just wanted to relax for a little bit. When the waitress came back for the order of food, I ordered another drink. Joe told the waitress that he would order, but don't bother with my food, because I preferred to drink my lunch. Again, I got insulted, and ordered a hamburger to save face. Then Joe told me that he had a bottle of vodka at his house that had been a gift and he hadn't opened it yet. I proceeded with as much subtlety as I could muster, to ask him how far he lived from where we were. He said he lived only about a mile from the diner. I told him I'd love to see his house and suggested that we buy some orange juice so I could make us a screwdriver while we viewed his home. He went for my idea and after paying the check, we rode to his house, which was really nice. He kept it spotlessly clean. He had brought the orange juice and I proceeded to make us some drinks. I used a shot glass for him and poured straight out of the bottle for me.

What made me think this day would be any different from the rest? We sat on his stoop and talked about different things in life that we both seemed to enjoy. I could certainly bullshit; I had been Queen of the Con in my day. We talked about nice things, like the home I would like someday with the white picket fence. All fairy tale stuff. He said that I could make some of these dreams come true, if only I would do something about my drinking. At that point, even being drunk, it was like someone believed in me. I told him that I had fought hard to stop drinking, but each battle ended in defeat. I said that maybe I would try harder, but I knew I couldn't do anything without a Divine intervention from a Higher Power. It has been said that "your as sick as your secrets" and I had plenty of them. There were a lot of things that I did while drinking that I didn't want him or anyone to know.

I fell asleep at his house and once again he didn't rape me or abuse me in any way. I even asked him if he was gay. I began to think he liked boys. But that wasn't the case. He told me he had two children, one boy and one girl. His son, Joey was almost my age. His daughter, Debbie lived with him, but she was away for that weekend. I stayed at his house all day and slept, while he went to work. He drove me home that night after he cooked me dinner, when he got home from work. He certainly was different from what I was used to, and I liked it. There was a kindness and gentleness about him. My son had stayed with Tessa and her kids overnight. At least I knew he was safe and I wasn't to worry, but Joe told me to call her to make sure everything was all right. I did call and talked to Marcus, who reassured me that he was fine, than I felt better.

Joe and I started a relationship, something I knew nothing about. Me, always promising to try to be sober when he got to my house. Most of the time failing and lying to him. He would call before he drove all the way from the shore area and I would say, "I only had one drink" He never believed me. He begged me to go to a hospital for help and I would promise, I even made the arrangements, but I would not go. Finally I called AA, and told whom ever I spoke to, that I needed help. That day, I got a call from a woman who asked me to meet her somewhere in Newark. I met the woman, who would become my sponsor, that night. She was a loving black woman who had gone through her own living hell, before getting sober. I was shaking like a leaf, in a storm., I needed a drink real bad. That day I tried to ease up on my drinking, because she made me promise to meet her. We took two buses, to get to the meeting that night. I thought I was going to die. I knew that the insane asylum lay ahead for me, so I didn't have any choices left. Plus the fact that I wanted to show Joe that I could do this. After the meeting this woman, Betty, shared her experience, strength, and hope with me. She suggested that I get to a meeting every day, for the first 90 days, then if I felt that I wasn't an alcoholic, she would refund my misery. She even suggested that I take a Valium if I got to shaky. Plus I would have a lot of money saved, to really tie one on. That night when I got home, I really needed a drink. I had hidden a bottle just in case this AA thing didn't work. I drank myself into oblivion that night, but everything I heard at that meeting plus what Betty had shared with me, seemed to get me thinking, something I hadn't done in a long time. The following night, I went to another meeting. Every time Joe would call, I told him I was going to a meeting. I couldn't believe that a whole month had passed and I hadn't had a drink. Even my neighbors were starting to talk to me. Joe had introduced me to his family, who accepted me as his girlfriend. He was real happy about my being sober, and wonderfully supportive.

I was beginning to believe that I wasn't hopeless or helpless like they had labeled me in A.A, and I had labeled myself years before. I even started driving a car again. When I was drinking I was a bounce-off-one-car-to-another drunk driver. That's when I got paranoid behind the wheel and stopped driving altogether. In this one month that I was sober, Joe got me behind the wheel and supported me to get me to drive. He also introduced me to his daughter's fiancé, a clothing wholesaler in New York, who thought I would be so good in sales that he backed me up with wholesale clothes to sell. The first week, I sold out all the clothes he had given me on a consignment basis. I had money in my pocket and couldn't wait to make more. Selling clothes was so exciting! I felt the same euphoria I felt when I gambled and drank.

I was still attending AA, but everything I was doing was so fast. I wanted what I wanted and I wanted it now. It all had to happen tomorrow. I learned too late, that I had to learn to crawl before I could walk. I felt that I had to take on all of life's difficult challenges in their entirety. The point is that I didn't have to. I found that the most burdensome tasks can be done one day at a time, or if that's too much, then one hour or even one moment at a time. Before I could step out and do anything, I was supposed to stop and ask my Higher Power for help and then let my conscience be my guide. I had been invited to go to an AA convention, some where in N.Y State, that weekend. I told everyone that I would go just for the one day, which was Sunday. Joe had called and asked me to go out riding with him on Saturday and I told him, no, that I was going to the convention the next morning, so I couldn't go. I was playing the martyr because he told me that he was still going riding with his friends and would see me in a few days. How dare he go and have a good time without me? I knew that I had stopped drinking for him, not for myself. I began to resent him for it. Resentment is reliving that feeling over and over, until it's grown out of proportation, and it eats you up. I went that Sunday, and I guess I had a good time, but I also knew that I wanted to drink again. On the way home from the convention, I had told the AA people that I was going to drink that night. They tried to talk to me, but I had already taken the drink mentally, so I knew I would have to take it physically, if I didn't get it out of my head. They told me to think it through, and to see how far I've come in this short time, but all that didn't phase me in the least. Again, the power of this disease is overwhelming. I know today that I tried to stay sober, for all the wrong reasons. A child, a man, a family that doesn't get you sober, or keep you sober. You need to do it for yourself. I needed a spiritual experience, in order to stay sober, but I still wasn't willing or able to turn my will and my life over to the care of God. as I understood Him. I felt that He had forsaken me and left me a long time ago because of my unworthiness. I had admitted publicly that I was powerless over alcohol and, that my life was unmanageable, but I didn't really believe it or accept it, therefore I couldn't surrender to it, and that's what I needed to do. After my AA friends tried to talk to me, I got out of the car and told them that I would try not to take that first drink. I knew by then that one drink was too much and a thousand wasn't enough. It was that first drink that would set off the compulsion and the mental obsession again. I walked up to the liquor store, knowing it was past 10pm and they would be closed. I was playing mind games again. I drove over to Tessa's house where my son was staying for the night. I was thinking about picking him up, so it might take my mind off the drink. When I got there, all the kids were in bed for the night, sleeping. I asked Tessa if she had anything to drink in the house. She said she had beer, but that I couldn't have any because I was sober and going to AA. I told her that the AA people said, after I was sober for a month, that I could have a few drinks. She believed me, because she had lost her drinking partner when I stopped and, even though she would say she hated when I drank the way I did, she missed me. Or maybe she really believed me, I'll never be sure. I remember taking only one beer from her and that terrible taste it put in my mouth. It had been one month since my last drink, so I was intoxicated right away.

The last beating

I barely remember leaving her house and getting in my car. I know that I drove down the street to the closest bar. I went in the bar and ordered a shot of whiskey. At which time a few guys tried right away to buy me a drink. I guess they saw that I was stoned already, so it wouldn't take much. Again, I blacked out and the next thing I remember was someone was beating me in my head and on my face. I barely remember them raping me after tying my hands behind my back. When, I came too, I was in my bed in my apartment, and didn't know how I got there. I got out of the bed, to find that I could hardly walk, I was full of blood, and I hurt all over. I went into the bathroom. I looked into the mirror by accident, and found that my face was all swollen and black and blue. My chest hurt so badly. When I looked at it, it was covered with blood, almost like someone had stomped on me with his shoes. My ribs hurt where I was kicked, over and over. I barely remember them putting a rope around my neck and dragging me through the ghetto area, calling me terrible names. I knew then that this was my destiny. This is what I deserved and this is the way I would die. I prayed to die that day. I asked God to take me out of this miserable world and give me peace. I was at the lowest point of my entire life. I felt very sorry for myself.

I had attempted suicide on several occasions, always making sure there was someone within reaching distance to see that I didn't finish the job. I would take a handful of pills or slash my wrists, but not cut too deep. Just enough to bleed all over everything, which looked worse than it was. I did believe that suicide was the worst one of God's laws to break, because God had given His only son, Jesus Christ, who died for us to have life. Somewhere in my alcoholic haze I remembered that. So, as bad as I wanted to die, I couldn't kill myself.

When I thought I was so beautiful in those days, towards the end, I can still see my hair half-bleached, not combed, this really added to my beauty. Then there are always the wrinkled slacks that have been slept in for days that could walk away by themselves, and the grimy sweater that we think we look so sexy in, even without a bra. And don't forget the runs in our stockings and the shoes are no better than a hobo's. Many of us remember our big mouths when it comes to a drink, but somewhere along the line, we forgot to take care of our teeth. This really makes for an attractive woman. I was only 29 years old and had lived through enough bad times in my lifetime to last me forever. This was not living; I just existed the only way I knew. I didn't analyze why this had happened to me, or why I was so different than my brother or sister. He was a good man and such a hard worker that he had a made a good life for him and his family. My sister, who had raised her 5 kids, mostly by herself after her alcoholic husband took off, was also a hard worker and did do the right thing in life to survive. She lived for those kids, who all grew up successful. Maybe because she taught them to work hard, like she did. So me, being the youngest, what happened to me? None else had gotten themselves locked up or lived in the ghetto of Newark, only me. The day after my beating, Joe called to see if he could come over that night after work. I told him I couldn't see him any more. He asked me if I was all right? He said I sounded funny. I guess when your mouth is split open, you do sound funny. I told him I had a cold. He asked how everything went at the convention. I told him it was all right. I told him I wanted to be left alone, and that I had thought about our relationship and everything was happening too fast, so I didn't want to see him for a while. I guess he didn't believe me, because within an hour and a half, he was ringing my doorbell.

Tessa had brought my son back to my apartment by this time and when she and my son saw me they both cried. They asked what had happened. I told them that I was in a car accident. Tessa went outside to check my car and came back in to tell me that all the windows in my car were busted out. The guys that beat me were not out just to wreck me, but my car as well. Next thing I knew, Joe was in my house. I had told my son to hide and don't answer the door, but he was afraid for me, so he opened it anyway. Joe took one look at me and almost fainted. He said he had been in the war and had not seen too many look as bad as I did. He begged me to let him take me to the hospital for x-rays, but I declined, saying that I would be all right. He went out to get my son and me something to eat, which was nice of him, but I couldn't eat. I told him that I had been in an accident, but he refused to believe me. I finally told him what I could remember, which wasn't much. I just wanted him to leave so I could try to get something to drink. I had once again accepted the fact that I was a chronic alcoholic and needed to drink in order to stay alive. Joe invited my son to his house for the Christmas holiday because my son was on winter break from school and he knew that I wasn't capable of taking care of him. He wanted me to go too, but I couldn't do that, I told him. Neither one of us went.

Christmas 1972

Christmas consisted of me, in a pair of hot pants, with a gallon of wine, dancing around a Christmas tree that wasn't put up right. My son opening some presents that I had brought him. As long as he had something to keep him busy, he stayed out of my way. I tried to cook a meal, but that was a disaster. I dropped the turkey on the floor, than scooped it up to set it on the table. I had told my son that I would make him real mashed potatoes, than found I didn't have any, so I made him some, pasty imitation potatoes. Then to top things off, I had become to drunk to eat anything, which hurt him deeply. He ate alone that Christmas. He was used to it by now. It was just like any other day, for him and me. My family had not spoken to me for a long time; so there wasn't any family get together. I was totally isolated from everyone and wanted it like that, or maybe I was just lying to myself, I'm not sure. I know I wished that my son could see his Aunt, Uncle and cousins sometimes. He missed his Grandpa, the most. He was settled down the shore and I didn't have the nerve to go there, I was too ashamed, of myself.

Somehow the winter came and went fast. I stayed in the house drinking around the clock, most of the time I didn't know whether it was day or night. Joe kept calling, but I was so paranoid again, that I couldn't answer the telephone. He would come to the apartment and I wouldn't let him in. After a while, he stopped coming. I got so bad; I was unable to walk anymore, I had alcohol arthritis in my legs and I had such bad pains in my stomach, from gastritis that I couldn't eat. Tessa got me to the City Hospital, to get treated, finally in the summer of 1972. The hospital arranged for me to go to the liver and alcohol clinic, which is in the hospital, twice a week, for treatment. This was some form of out patient clinic for alcoholics. They said I was suffering from acute alcoholism. . (So what else was new?) At the clinic, I watched many people go into alcoholic convulsions, where they had to have something placed under their tongue, in order not to swallow it. As much as I saw these things happen to other people at the clinic, I guess I figured it would never happen to me. They say, "Nothing scares an alcoholic."

As an indication of just how sick, confused and mixed up I was, just as soon as I got to the clinic, I would hurry around to tell the other patients and the nursing staff that I was getting better. I had been a chronic alcoholic, now I just suffered from acute alcoholism. I honestly didn't know the difference. AA didn't teach me that I was an alcoholic; rather it taught me that because I was an alcoholic my life had become unmanageable, as I was to learn later. I knew, that only a Power greater than myself could restore me to sanity. I needed to surrender totally, but I wasn't sure how to do that.

It's a wonder that the Welfare Department never removed my son from me and put him in foster care. I loved the boy, but I was certainly an unfit mother. They had tried once, when I had hit him while in a blackout and my friend Tessa called the police. They arrested me and put me in jail for the night to sober up. The next day I told the judge that I would never do it again, so he let me go. Marcus wasn't hurt, except for a bloody nose. Welfare never said anything to me about it that I can remember. I knew my 8year old son was suffering as a result of my drinking and, at age 29, I felt that my life was over and I just wanted to die. My family had deserted me, or I them, because no one could understand why I had become the person I now was. I had one friend left, Tessa, who was trying to cut off my liquor supply, so there weren't any options left. I knew I had to do whatever was necessary to try to get my life in some kind of order.

Getting Sober

*O*n *June 26,1973* I packed up the car, the one without the windows and drove us down to the seashore. I was so sick from drinking that I didn't drink anything before I left. It's in creditable that the police for having no windshield didn't stop me. When we were almost to Joe's house, I told my son that I was going to stop for just one drink at a bar. I could see the terror in his eyes and he started to cry, but I told him I would get him a bag of chips and a soda and he seemed to be all right with that. An hour before, I had told him that our lives were going to change, because Mommy was going to stop drinking. I had my one drink and got back in the car with him. I knew that once I got to Joe's house that I had to do what was right. I knew he wouldn't tolerate my behavior. When we got there, Joe was so happy to see us. I fell out of the car into his waiting arms. Joe had got a schedule of AA meetings in the area from the yellow pages. Boy! He had me all set up. He put me to bed, to rest for a while so I could drive his car to the meeting that night. I knew I had to go by myself and for myself, if I was going to make it. It says in Matthew 21:22 "All things, whatsoever ye shall ask in prayer, believing, ye shall receive." I had to trust and believe that I was going to be all right.

While I was getting dressed and ready to go to the meeting, my legs and hands were shaking so hard, I didn't think I would be able to drive. I was going on blind faith and knew I couldn't turn back. I only had a few blocks to go, to get to the meeting. At times when faced

with especially difficult tasks, I have contemplated the enormity of
what lies ahead, my projections often told me that I couldn't possibly
make it through, even though I would feel thoroughly persuaded
that I would fall short of any positive goals, and that my negative
convictions would become a self-fulfilling prophecy. I got in the car
and, as I was driving, I was looking to see if there were any bars
around, just in case I changed my mind. Oddly enough, there was a
bar almost across the street from the meeting. I had figured that I
would play this game until I felt better, then I would go back to my
project apartment, and drink my wine, hopefully until I died.

I walked into the meeting early, the people greeted me with
love and concern, easily seeing the bad shape I was in. I even helped
them set up the coffee and put the chairs out. After the meeting,
the people gave me their phone numbers and a meeting book and
suggested that I make a meeting every day, for 90 days. Then, if I felt
that I didn't belong there, they would refund my misery.

I went back to Joe's house full of hope, maybe I could get
honest with myself, without any hidden agendas or motives. I'd have
to think about that. The next day Joe took me to his doctor to get me
a B12 shot because my body was craving a drink and I couldn't stop
shaking. The doctor suggested that I take some sedatives to help
with my withdrawal. I decided that I needed to remember the pain,
of going "cold turkey." I didn't want the easy way out, so I refused
any medication. Instead, I drank a lot of orange juice and ate honey,
which helped, because it had the sugar I needed to replace the sugar
from the booze. The doctor told me that this would help me with
the shakes from the withdrawal. He also said that a person could die
during withdrawal because it's a strain on your heart and I could have
gone into convulsions, but I didn't. I do know today that it's easier to
stay sober, than it is to get sober.

Well, as the days and meetings went by, I started to feel much
better, but I still couldn't get honest with myself or other people.
I was still conniving about taking a drink. Always thinking about
when I could take that first one again. Things were too calm, and
boring for me. I was used to and missed my chaotic lifestyle. Chapter

5 in the Alcoholics Anonymous says that there are people who suffer from grave emotional and mental disorders, but if they have the capacity to be honest, they can also recover. I still had my doubts. Even the people I had met in AA told me that it appeared that I was constitutionally incapable of grasping and developing a manner of living which demands rigorous honesty. I had met a wonderful woman, Kay, who I had asked to be my sponsor. I figured I'd play the game and make it look good. She was not like me whatsoever. She appeared to be the perfect young lady type. Her bottom was drinking one bottle of wine a week. I certainly couldn't identify with that. I told her that if that were all I drank, I wouldn't have a problem. She said, "It's not what you drink or how much you drink, it's what that first drink does to you to make your life unmanageable."

The accident

I had come to realize that something was happening that was impossible without the help of God. It was clear that a Power greater than myself was keeping me from drinking. On August 1st 1973, with over thirty days sober, I decided that I needed to go back to Newark, to get my welfare check and maybe I would get something to drink while I was there. Who would know? I thought I had surrendered to my disease but I didn't. I still had "stinking thinking" and some reservations that I couldn't let go of. As I was leaving Joe's house that morning, with my son in the car, my intentions were not good. Joe was right behind me because he was going to work. He had made me promise that I wouldn't drink anything when I got to Newark. Well, promises didn't mean anything to me, anyway. I wasn't ready to accept that I couldn't drink anymore. Maybe just one! I never made it back to Newark that day. I no sooner got on the highway, when a car, that was traveling too fast, hit me and threw my car into a telephone pole. Joe later told me that the police had to cut the top of the car off to get us out. I awoke the next day in the hospital. My son was also there, down the hall from me. He had a broken leg and a lot of contusions. As for me, I had plates and screws put in my arm and my face was hideous looking, because I was under the dashboard of the car when they, got me out. While I lay in the hospital, my sponsor and other AA friends came to see me. Some of them cried, because of the way I looked. My first thoughts were, what do they want? I had nothing to give them. I finally realized

that they loved me, because I was one of them and they wanted
nothing from me. They were there to give me something that I could
hang on to get me through this perilous time with their love and
understanding. That started my journey into my recovery. Having
never had the chance to go through rehabilitation, or detoxification,
this was the first time that I was dried out and was able to really think
about what I needed to do about my life. It's terrible to lose your best
friend, mine being alcohol, and to wonder about how your going to
live without it. What would take away those feeling of desperation,
bitterness, remorse and fear? I knew that society could do anything
it chooses to me when I was drunk and I can't lift a finger to stop
it, for I forfeit my rights through the simple expedient of becoming
a menace to myself and those around me. I needed the willingness
to change, and stop making excuses for my lack of education, my
personal failures, my inadequacy, and of course my alcoholism. I had
lost most of my faith through my years of drinking, but I came to
believe that a Power greater than myself could restore me to sanity.
Every morning I got down on my knees and asked God to point
out to me some way to stop the resentments, the hate, and to help
me with my character defeats. I needed to take a fearless moral
inventory of my self, to right some of the wrongs that I had done
before I could get my life straight. My major defects–the so-called
Seven Deadly Sins, of pride, greed, lust, anger, gluttony, envy, and
sloth. It is not by any accident that pride, headed the procession. For
pride, leading to self-justification, and always spurred by conscious
or unconscious fears, is the basic breeder of most human difficulties,
the block to true progress. The AA people told me that if I would ask
in prayer for the people I resented to have everything that I wanted
for myself to be given to them, than I would be free from it. Where I
used to feel bitterness and resentment and hatred, I would now feel
compassionate understanding and love. It worked for me than and
has worked many times since. This great experience that released me
from the bondage of hatred and replaced it with love is just another
affirmation of the truth I know today. All my life I was looking for
something through the bottom of a bottle. Every thing I ever wanted

or needed in life, was right there in front of me all the time. I just didn't trust that God loved me enough to provide for me. After I got released from the hospital, along with my son, I started going to the meetings every night. I couldn't drive because my arm was still in a cast, but I got on the phone and called everyone until I got someone who could pick me up. My desire to get honest with myself made it necessary for me to realize that sometimes, even now, was irrational. It had to be or I could not have justified my erratic behavior as I did. I looked up the word in the dictionary, it read: "rationalization is giving a socially acceptable reason for socially unacceptable behavior, and socially unacceptable behavior is a form of insanity." I had to admit that I was powerless over alcohol—that my life had become unmanageable. Admission of powerlessness is the first step in liberation. All those years I would say, "I'll try tomorrow." I accepted the fact that the mental obsession, plus the physical allergy, made me a full-blown alcoholic. It would take time to surrender to this disease and that could not happen until I came to believe that a Power greater than myself could restore me to sanity. That was the rallying point to sanity and it started my new relationship with God. I was told by my sponsor to "Make a decision to turn my will and my life over to the care of God as I understand Him." This step is like the opening of the locked door. Willingness is the key. I had tried it my way now I was ready to try it His way. I had to get active in the AA program. I was told that I had to die in order to live. They also said that once I get it, I had to give it away, in order to keep it. Which meant, that I had to share my experience, strength and hope with others who were struggling with their sobriety. When I had first heard others talk about God, it seemed that each person's concept was unlike that of every other person's concept. However when I stopped comparing differences and began listening for similarities, I realized they all perceived God as part of them. That idea had great appeal to me. All this time I was attempting to fill a spiritual void with material possessions, grandiose behaviors, and acting like a big shot, false pride and anger. When all I needed to do was fill myself with God and all good things would come. I had become discouraged when I perceived happiness as something you either have in its entirety or not at all. When I was able to seriously examine my beliefs and misconceptions, I realized that happiness comes during moments in a day, not as a "forever" thing. I began to savor the individual moments and was surprised at how many there actually were: the satisfaction of a job well done; the sense of deep understanding with a friend; and the beauty of a sunrise. Even the most miraculous changes manifest themselves a new day at a time. Incalculable are the intangible initiation fee that I had paid: the sick, sick hangovers, the bitter remorse, guilt, broken home, jail and the mental anguish in general that had been generated over the years. But, now with His grace and help, this child of His has paid this initiation fee for good. Spiritually... I found a Friend who never lets me down. I actually take my problems to Him and He gives me comfort, peace, and happiness. I have become grateful for all my days and the blessings that I had overlooked for so many years. When I see people who are having a hard time getting sober, I always remember, "But for the Grace of God, there go I." Today I have a spiritual tool kit to solve all the problems of living. You can't think your way out of this disease and it makes no difference why. I am an alcoholic. It makes all the difference knowing that I am one. I stay sober because I've had a spiritual awakening, as a result of working the twelve steps of AA and practicing their principles in all my affairs. At lest the best that I can. I will never be perfect, but can strive for spiritual gains on a daily basis. I was no longer obsessing about ways to drink, instead, I find myself thinking of ways to stay sober. I found that God does love me, and all His children, regardless of our sins, long as we're willing to make a covenant with Him. He had restored me to sanity; He removed the compulsion to drink and the mental obsession from my body. Soon after I learned to "Let go and Let God" take over my will and my life to the best of my ability. Anything that I could do about a certain problem, I could do and leave the rest to my Higher Power. Giving up alcohol alone was not enough for me; I had to give up all mood and mind affecting chemicals in order to stay sober and comfortable.

90 days sober

When I was sober 90 days, I was crying with happiness. It was one of the best days of my life. My sponsor gave me a pin that said; "To thine own self be true; Unity, Fellowship and Honesty." She also gave me a book that helped me change my life. It was a cross reference between the Bible and the AA program. That book was *The Power of Positive Thinking* by Norman Vincent Peale. How I ever had felt that God was against me, I'll never know. I believe that He had a plan for me all this time. He made me live through what I did, in order to get me where I am today. My past became my greatest asset in working with others. I had gotten to be an active member of my home group, where I picked up ashtrays, made coffee and went on speaking commitments to other groups, to carry the message of sobriety. I started to sponsor other women alcoholics who were just coming into the program. The men with the men and the women with the women. There's a reason for that. We are so vulnerable, when we're new, that when someone is nice to us we think they want something from us. Also, it's too easy to get emotionally involved when you're new and want someone to care about you.

Getting Married

When I was sober two years, I married Joe, my sweet, supportive, wonderful man. We had a big wedding and invited my whole AA family. My brother and sister still didn't bother with me yet, so they weren't there. My father lived out of town and couldn't get there, but he sent his blessings. I got married in a nice white gown, which Joe insisted on. We got married in the church, which we had attended for the past year, by our Pastor. I had been baptized for the first time in my life and was certainly born again. We went all out for our wedding, with flowers, ushers, bride's maids, a best man and a matron of honor. My son was the ring bearer, along with a flower girl, who was his age. For the first time in his eight young years he had a father and mother who he could love and respect. It was a happy, wonderful day for everyone. We didn't have much money, but everyone helped out by cooking food for the reception. We even had a band and danced the night away. I believe that was the first time I danced sober. All those go-go outfits that I hung on to for a while, just in case, I had worn one to my first AA Halloween costume party, than I finally decided to throw them out.

Faith by its nature is mysterious. We need only know that it works. I really had to always look at my motives for doing some of the things I did. Old habits die-hard. I couldn't afford the price of having excess baggage. Character flaws need not be permanent, but they can be "named, claimed, and dumped."

It was my first marriage and Joe's second. He had been married

20 years to his first wife, who I got to know and got along well with. She had been remarried to another guy, who was a good cook and they would invite us to their home for dinner quite often. After our wedding we went on our honeymoon. One thing that I still dealt with was my lack of being able to be intimate. I wasn't a very loving sexual person, even in my marriage. Those walls stayed up regardless of how much I cared or trusted. Maybe in my heart I'll never get over that. I've spoken to doctors, and counselors, who agreed that something dramatic happened in my childhood or when I was drinking that, had affected me, that way. I had heard other women talk about themselves, feeling the same way, so it isn't too rare.

A baby girl

When I was married three years, and sober five years, one of my many miracles happened. I found out that I was pregnant. I never thought in a million years that this would happen. Everything in God's world happens how and when it is supposed to. I didn't think I could ever have any more children after what I had gone through in my lifetime. This opened my heart and mind to a new sense of wholeness and equality. It was surely another one of God's miracles, happening in our lives. Joe's children were already grown and he was also a grandfather, by this time. My son was now almost 14 years old. There was a time in my life when I would scoff at the very idea of miracles. There are days that I am literally astonished to be alive. When I think back to the constantly perilous existence I led—and to the times I was close to death, from the severe beatings I took—I am filled with gratitude just to be breathing, let alone to have physical and mental capabilities. Out of the true miracle of my sobriety today flows a host of other miracles. I am the same person I was back than to be sure, but I feel differently about myself. My self-loathing has been replaced with a sense of self-respect and usefulness. Today I am aware that all of this has come to pass only because of the power and Grace of God. To know that you yourself is a miracle a believe you can make miracles happen by thinking, praying, working and by helping other people. That awareness for me is perhaps the greatest gift of all. For me, AA is a synthesis of all the philosophy I've ever read, all the positive, good philosophy, all of it is based on love. By the end of January, the doctor said he would have to induce the baby with two weeks, because of the complications I had. High blood pressure, toxemia, basically the same problems I had with Marcus. My doctor asked me to pick the date. I said I wanted the baby to be born on Valentines Day. On Feb 14,1978, the doctor started to induce the baby, it wouldn't come. I went through hell trying to push it out, but it wouldn't come down I felt like I was going to die. The next day, the nurses started the inducement process again. It was real early in the morning The doctor said if the baby didn't come by 12pm, that he would have to take it Caesarean. My husband was in the room with me and begged the doctor not to take it like that if at all possible. On February 15, 1978, at 12:05 pm, I had a baby girl. She was 6lbs. 14oz., 20 inches long. We named her Dina Maria. She was the little baby doll I never had as a kid. She was the most beautiful thing I ever seen, since my son was born. From that first few moments, it was unconditional love. I nursed her because I had heard that it was healthier. There was a closeness that I never felt in my life. My song to her was "You light up my life" and I would hold her tight to me and sing to her every day. I was now thirty-five years old, and Joe was fifty-six. He was already a grandfather. It had been fourteen years since I had my son, and for Joe it was twenty-six years between children. I knew I could get through this new adventure, because my son and husband were always there when I needed them.

I had come to love my son deeply, but felt bad for a long time about the way I had treated him when I was drinking. I had read that "If God be for you, who can be against you?" That passage helped me to forgive myself for all the wrongs I had done to him, only then could I start to make amends to him, one day at a time. Time goes by so quickly when you're busy doing good things instead of always being on the "pity pot." I never had much schooling; so I got my GED without any trouble and went to Cosmetology School, while I carried my baby until the seventh month when I had to leave. I went back to complete my hours at night, after I had my baby and passed my cosmetology State Boards. My son was a gem. He watched his sister and never complained. He loved her with all his heart and took excellent care of her. He would change her diapers and call her "stink in the pants." When he had his own child, I'll bet he said the same thing to her. The cage within me, where I stuffed my painful feelings, started to become the cage around me. I knew I needed something more. When I told Joe that I wanted to go to college to study fashion, he wasn't happy about it. He would much rather me stay home and keep doing what I had been doing. I had been selling clothes out of my house and car for a few years and it was a profitable business. I wanted a college diploma, more than I wanted anything. It's a shame that I had to leave him to do it, but I knew I couldn't go to school five days a week, study and be a good wife.

Starting College

I desperately needed some polish in my life and I felt that it would come through education. I was too rough around the edges. It wasn't easy going to school everyday and leaving my daughter in the day care program. I sold clothes that I would bring in from N.Y and mark them up only a few dollars and sell them real fast. This had turned into a profitable business; I made a good living from it. I studied Fashion Merchandising and did my internship in my own business, which was great. When I did graduate two years later, Joe was there to cry with me over this achievement, even though it had cost us our marriage. We had been separated for those two years and our divorce was final that year, 1984, but we are good friends and still loved and respected each other in our own way. I continued to work in my own clothing business, which was successful for many years. I have had some harsh days put in front of me and still do sometimes, but there has been nothing I that I couldn't get through clean and sober.

By honestly assessing my capabilities and special needs, I came to build self-confidence. I tried to practice the Serenity Prayer everyday in my life: "God grant me the serenity to Accept the things I cannot change, the Courage to change the things I can, and the Wisdom to know the difference." What powerful words!

When I was sober almost 20 years, a girl I sponsored called to tell me that a girl she sponsored lived in a house she rented from a guy named Archie, with the same last name as my old probation officer in Newark. My sponsee called his business phone that was given to her and found that he was my ex-probation officer. I received a call the next day saying that he had gotten the message and was shocked to find out it was about me. He had thought about me many times over the last 23 years and believed that I had to be dead by now. He also said he heard from my sponsee that I was ready to celebrate my 20th anniversary that month on June 27,1993. He asked me the name of the town, and which meeting was I celebrating at, I told him Belford, N.J. He said he'd find me, and he did. He came to help me celebrate. We knew each other at first glance. He said I had gained a little weight, but looked healthy. We talked for hours after the meeting and I cried out of gratitude for all those years he had tried to help me. It had to be a miracle for this to happen. I may never see him again but to have the one time opportunity to say "thank you" is something I'll always remember.

MY SON

My son is a man now, 36 years old, married with two daughters. They are so beautiful. He married a lovely girl who is the perfect understanding wife. I couldn't have hand picked her better myself. She stood by him and worked hard, while he went on to graduate from college with a B.A degree in philosophy and became a secure business owner. They have worked very hard to achieve the kind of life they have today. He is also an active member of AA and has been sober 16 years. I've always believed that he was genetically predisposed to become an alcoholic, that if these people go through a period in their lives of heavy drinking, that some kind of "switch" is permanently turned on in their brain that makes them no longer able to ever drink in moderation. He knew where to go, when his life had become unmanageable due to alcohol. I had never seen him drink, he hid it well. The seed had been planted at an early age. I am so very grateful that he got sober, when he did, so he didn't have to endure anymore pain and suffering that he did at such an early age. Those in A.A say it is " attraction rather than promotion."

TESSA

Tessa, who I always had thought about through the years, had begun to drink more and hit the skids after I left Newark. She was drinking real hard and working as a barmaid. She had met a guy who was a truck driver, who traveled all over the States. He befriended her and her children. He was a born again Christian. They got together and they got married after she accepted Jesus as her Savior. We had seen each other after almost twenty-six years, because her son Charlie got in touch with me. She drove to New Jersey from Texas to visit me on June 20,1999. It was such a wonderful day for both of us. She had been sober for five years. I told her about how A.A works and the 12 steps of the program. She said she was going to go to some meetings, when she went back home. She felt she needed to start working with other addicts to insure her sobriety, because she realized that is what was missing from her life. I suggested she work with addicts in her ministry. I had told her that A.A was not a religious program, but a spiritual program. She left to go back to Texas with a lot of hope and knowledge about A.A and with the Big Book (Alcoholics Anonymous) in hand. My family and loved ones, all my friends, my sponsor Kay H. is nearer and dearer to me than ever before. She had moved to Texas a few years ago, but we stay in touch. My friend, Jeanie, who taught me that you don't have to be an alcoholic to have bad things happen to you. I have literally dozens of new friends who say they cannot believe that I'm the same person I talk about when I speak at meetings today. I have seen that there is only one law, the law of love, and there are only two sins, the first is to interfere with the growth of another human being and the second is to interfere with one's own growth. I even opened a restaurant, and named it the Serenity Café, after the Serenity Prayer. I had so many drunks coming in for coffee that, to make any money, I had to close it up and get a job.

CERTIFIED ALCOHOL
AND DRUG COUNSELOR

I have been a counselor for many years now, working with alcoholics, drug addicts and the mentally ill population. I have just received my certification after many years of not wanting it. The whole reason behind this was that I always believed in my heart, that what was given to me freely, let me give back freely. Being a counselor wasn't my chosen profession, until I decided that who was better qualified to work with another alcoholic, than I. What is more, my growing self-honesty has shown me never to be judgmental of another person; this flaw interferes with the development of such qualities as tolerance, understanding and kindness. Most of the time we judge because we don't really know anything about that person, what they've had to endure and overcome to get to where they are now. If anyone had judged me when I was getting sober I wouldn't have stayed around long enough to stay sober. When I remember the unconditional love that was given to me so freely and the acceptance, before I could love or accept myself, it is truly remarkable. It has been a wonderful journey. Working with others has been the key to my staying sober. To see people who are new in AA, to feel the pain and suffering that they are going through, keeps my memory green. First, I had to "get it" than I had to give it away, in order to keep it! It keeps me from forgetting where I came from and where I'll go back to, if I was to pick up that first drink. I have seen many people die over the years from this disease and I have seen many people live because they got sober. I was re-born on June 27,1973. That day I got sober, at 30 years old. I think the hardest part of working this program was to come to a place of "acceptance" that sobriety is the only road for me to follow. Today, I'm fifty-eight years old; my life is so filled with love and joy as a result of staying sober these twenty-eight years. It's been a long time between drinks! I used to say, " If only I could live my life over, knowing what I know now." I have been given that chance.

MY DAUGHTER

My daughter is now twenty-three years old. She was the missing link in my life; she is the wind beneath my wings on many days. She has been able to show me what being a mother is all about. Even being a sober mother isn't always an easy job. My father passed away many years ago, on November 22, 1997, but I was able to be with him till his last breath, unlike my mother. He had seen me sober many years before he left us, and had told me some of the reasons we lived as we had. He had accepted Jesus Christ as his Lord and Savior, long before he died. He attended church every week and was a good Christian. We had made our amends to each other. I could not afford the price of excess emotional baggage in my new life. There is no more "aloneness" with that awful ache, so deep in the heart of every alcoholic that nothing before, could ever reach it. That ache is gone for many years and need never to return. Now, there is a sense of belonging, and of being loved and cared about. In return for the remorse, bitterness, hate and the hangovers, I have been given peace of mind and serenity that has opened the door to my being teachable and willing to discover a new way of life. There isn't any more fear of what tomorrow will bring. If I do the right thing today, chances are that tomorrow will take care of it self. Today I try to wear the world as a loose garment. I am certain that as long as I'm willing to learn from my so-called failures, I can be assured of many successes. My worst day sober is much better than my best day drunk. When I forgave God for not being there for me, the healing begun. It wasn't Him that removed himself from me; it was I who turned away from Him. I haven't written this book hoping for a best seller. I certainly wouldn't mind making some money, for I'm not that humble, yet. I wrote it hoping to touch the life of another person who might read it and be able to identify in some way. Maybe they will not have to go the same route. I sincerely hope I have been able to impart to you, the reader, at least a bit of what I know, the struggles of life and the journey to hope and recovery. I'll always be an alcoholic no matter how long I'm sober. The disease is arrested for now. I have a daily reprieve, every day—one day at a time. I am truly a grateful alcoholic.

ABOUT THE AUTHOR

Jeanie L. is a 58-year old divorced mother of two children. She is a first time author who has written her compelling life story based on her battle with alcohol and drugs. She started to volunteer with alcoholics in 1974, one year after getting sober. She went on to become a Certified Alcoholism and Drug Counselor. She has worked in detoxification units, rehabilitation centers,and halfway houses. She served on the Board of Directors for Monmouth County Alcohol and Drug Abuse for eight years. The Monmouth County Division of Social Services employed her for nine years to work with the indigent alcoholic, drug abuser and the mentally ill chemical abuser, in their homes or on the streets. She has spoken in jails, reform schools,prisons, hospitals and many A.A meetings. She continues to work with addiction in her community,attending A.A meetings and is active in her church for the past twenty-eight years of sobriety. Jeanie L. has an Assiociate degree from Brookdale College and seventeen years of training in alcohol and drug studies. She lives with her daughter,Dina Marie, her dog, Tasha and her cat,Elvis in New Jersey.

ABOUT GREATUNPUBLISHED.COM

greatunpublished.com is a website that exists to serve writers and readers, and remove some of the commercial barriers between them. When you purchase a greatunpublished.com title, whether you receive it in electronic form or in a paperback volume or as a signed copy of the author's manuscript, you can be assured that the author is receiving a majority of the post-production revenue. Writers who join greatunpublished.com support the site and its marketing efforts with a per-title fee, and a portion of the site's share of profits are channeled into literacy programs.

So by purchasing this title from greatunpublished.com, you are helping to revolutionize the publishing industry for the benefit of writers and readers.
And for this we thank you.

3607271